Circle Time

ABC

Written by Susan Finkel and Karen Seberg

Illustrated by Gary Mohrman

Teaching & Learning Company

1204 Buchanan St., P.O. Box 10
Carthage, IL 62321-0010

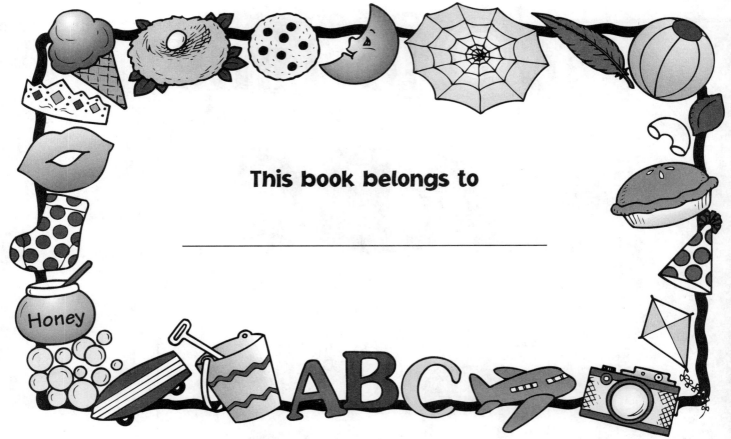

This book belongs to

_____

Special thanks to Building Blocks Child Care Center in Burlington, Iowa, for all of their help with the cover photograph. We had a blast!

The activity portrayed on the front cover is described on page 21.

Cover photo by Images and More Photography

ISBN No. 1-57310-097-8

Printing No. 987654321

Teaching & Learning Company
1204 Buchanan St., P.O. Box 10
Carthage, IL 62321-0010

Table of Contents

Every reasonable attempt has been made to identify copyrighted material.

Dear Teacher or Parent,

How often have you said these words *OK, everyone, time for circle time. Let's gather on the rug!* and then thought to yourself "What should we do today?" This book will help you through those times when you are tired of the same old ideas. We've taken many familiar children's songs and created some great circle time activities for you to try. In addition, we'll give you ideas for originating your own songs, using these familiar tunes.

What is circle time?
Circle times are large or small group gatherings. During your circle time, you may present daily or weekly themes or concepts. You may use books, pictures, flannel boards, concrete materials, share experiences and sing songs!

What is the best way to do circle time?
There is no "best" way. Each teacher has his or her own style. You can gather ideas for your circle times by reading books, attending classes and observing other teachers. Eventually, you will develop your own style, what works best for you and your class. Be aware that you may need to adjust your style from year to year, or even as the school year progresses, depending on the changes in your children.

Some circle time hints:
Establish a set place in your classroom to gather. It should be out of the room's main traffic pattern. A round or oval rug makes a great visual cue for the children as they come together. If possible, locate your circle time space near a window.

Have an easel, chalkboard or flannel board nearby for using visual aids or recording the children's ideas.

If you prefer a "backup" when you sing, use a tape, CD or record player. You don't need to be a great singer to have great circle times, but you will need to know how to use this equipment.

Plan your circle times for the same time each day. Children need a consistent schedule for each day's activities; they feel security in knowing the sequence of a day's planned events. Create a consistent pattern of activities within your circle time as well.

Name your circle time whatever you wish: morning meeting, group time, together time or something else unique to your children.

Use concrete items whenever possible.

If you find the children are not responding to a particular activity or song, STOP. Try again later, on another day or in another way.

Sincerely,

Susan Finkel and Karen Seberg

About This Book

Circle times are an important part of the early learner's day. The attachment young children develop to routine is supported with daily or regular circle time experiences. The socialization with daily or regular circle time settings are important acquisitions. The value of shared group experiences is evident in the opportunities presented to each child to contribute as an individual and participate as a member of a team. Plus circle times are great occasions to relax, learn, have some fun and–SING!

The circle times in this book use familiar children's songs as a starting point for many theme-related activities. (You may find the songs have regional variations.) Included for each song are its words and some of the following activities or suggestions: visuals, manipulatives and concrete objectives; actions and movements; variations; art and sensory activities; discussion ideas; changes in the classroom environment; sources of recorded versions.

Young children should be exposed to the alphabet, sounds and words in a variety of ways and throughout the school day. You may use the circle times in this book in any order–as your class learns a particular song or to correspond to a theme or unit. You might also choose to work through the book in alphabetical order, focusing on each letter for a week or two at a time.

Each circle time includes extra activities to reinforce the selected letter. Following are general activities that may be used for any letter of the alphabet.

Use the clip art provided for each letter to make domino games, file folder sorting activities and picture and/or word card matching activities. Color and cut out pictures to make borders for your letter bulletin board or hang them in mobiles. Enlarge or reduce the pictures on a photocopy machine to make a variety of sizes. Create big books with the large illustrations and invite the children to dictate sentences to correspond to the pictures. You might use smaller illustrations to make individual books for each child.

Have children bring to circle time items that begin with the selected letter. Create a class list of all the things that begin with the letter.

Invite parents and children to work together to circle the selected letter each time it appears on your class newsletter or calendar. Have them return the newsletter to school and compare the results.

Help the children learn to identify the sound of the selected letter by inviting them to clap hands or stomp feet when they hear the letter in a story, song or fingerplay.

Snack items are listed for each letter. Please be aware of any food allergies or restrictions your children may have before offering any of these items to your class.

Braille

Are You Awake?

To the tune of "Are You Sleeping?"
Are you awake, are you awake,
Brother John, Brother John?
Turn off the alarm clock! Turn off the alarm clock!
Buzz, buzz, buzz! Buzz, buzz, buzz!

Talk About

Sing this song at the first circle time of the day, using the names of the children in your group. Ask, "Who is the first person awake at your house?" Make a bar graph depicting family members and mark who is usually the first to rise in each child's family. Ask, "What do you do when you awake? How do you know when you are awake? What do you do when you fall asleep? How do you know you are asleep?"

Props/Visual Aids

Make copies of the pairs of eyes on page 8. Cut out and color each pair. On the backs of the matching pairs, write an uppercase letter and the matching lowercase letter. Mix the cards and invite the children to match the pairs of eyes. Do the letters on the backs match, too?

To Extend This Circle Time

If your program includes a nap or rest time, circulate through the room and sing this song to the children when it is time to wake up.

"Aiken Drum"
"Animal Crackers"
"The Ants Go Marching"
"Apples and Bananas"
"I Went to the Animal Fair"

almonds
angel food cake
apple butter
apples
applesauce
appetizers
apricots
avocados

Additional Activities

It is very important that children memorize their **addresses**. Write the address of each child in your class on a 3" x 5" (8 x 13 cm) card. Use the cards as flash cards with the group. Have each child stand when his or her address card is shown. Post a map of your community on the wall and find the home address of each of the children. Put a star sticker on each child's home, and write the street address on the map.

Advertisements are everywhere. Discuss the purpose of advertisements and invite the children to bring in newspaper or magazine ads for a bulletin board display. Videotape a few appropriate television ads to share with the children. Then create your own class advertisements either in print or on videotape. For example: "Drinking milk will help you grow strong bones, to help you run fast and climb high! Drink milk every day."

An **agenda** is a list of things to do or topics to be discussed in a meeting. Create an agenda for your circle time. Invite the children to list the items that are on the agenda every day and others that are special occurrences such as birthday celebrations.

Take a field trip to a nearby **airport**. Have any of the children ridden in an airplane? Was it large or small? Talk about the different types of airplanes you see and the different uses. Try to arrange for the children to see inside or board one of the airplanes.

Create a class **album** and add to it throughout the year. Include photographs, art projects, stories and special events. Be sure to have each child **autograph** a page in the album! Keep the album in an accessible place for easy additions and for parents' enjoyment!

Books to Share

Demuth, Patricia Brennan. *Those Amazing Ants.* Macmillan Publishing Company, 1994. Detailed illustrations and text describe how ants live, what they eat and some fascinating facts–such as ants nap, yawn and stretch!

Paschkis, Julie. *So Sleepy; Wide Awake.* Henry Holt and Company, 1994. In this clever book, the first half tells about sleepy animals. Turn the book upside down to read about animals when they are wide awake.

Rogers, Paul. *Somebody's Awake.* Atheneum, 1989. Mom and Dad can hear that somebody is awake downstairs, somebody who brightens their morning with a special surprise.

Russo, Marisabina. *Time to Wake Up!* Greenwillow Books, 1994. Bright paintings illustrate this story of a mom and her son as they wake up and get ready for the day.

Sendak, Maurice. *Alligators All Around.* HarperCollins Publishers, 1962. Alligators romp on every page of this humorous alphabet book.

Winn, Chris. *Archie's Acrobats.* Gollancz Children's Paperbacks, 1989. Archie's Amazing Acrobats are beginners, specializing in balancing acts, and they want to join a proper circus. Humorous illustrations depict Archie's many ideas for impressing Mr. Pedderfettle's World Famous Circus.

Tapes and CDs

Beall, Pamela Conn, and Susan Hagen Nipp. "The Ants Go Marching" from *Wee Sing Silly Songs.* Price Stern Sloan, 1986.

Lehman, Peg. "Aiken Drum" from *Critters in the Choir.* Pal Music, 1989.

Raffi. "Apples and Bananas" from *One Light, One Sun.* Troubadour Records, 1985.

Rosenthal, Phil. "Are You Sleeping?" from *The Paw Paw Patch.* American Melody Records, 1987.

Roth, Kevin. "Are You Sleeping?" from *Lullabies for Little Dreamers.* CMS Records, Inc., 1985.

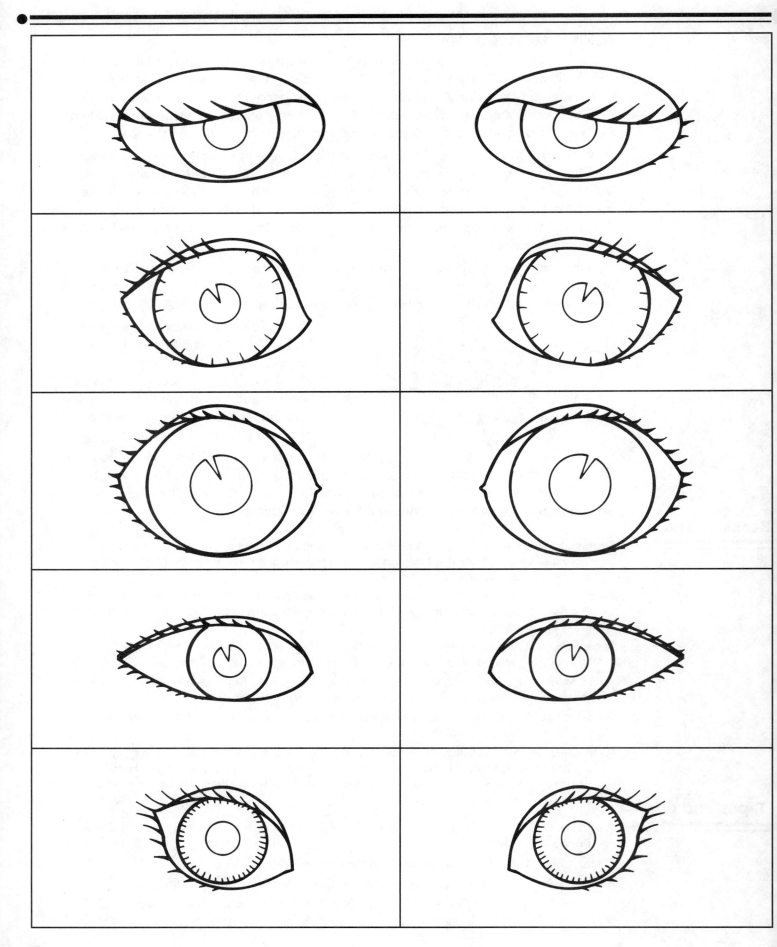

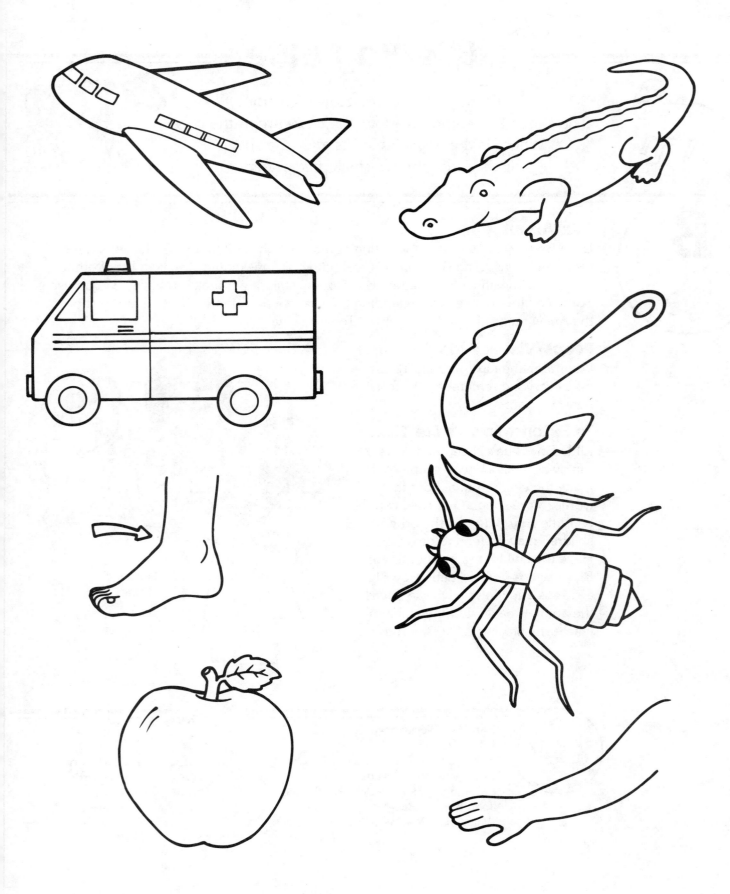

B

Little Boy Blue

Little Boy Blue, come blow your horn.
The sheep are in the meadow, the cows are in the corn.
Where is the boy who looks after the sheep?
He's under the haystack, fast asleep!

Talk About
Little Boy Blue has a very interesting name! Ask the children how they think he got his name. Was *Little Boy Blue* his real name or a nickname? Make a list of other names that begin with the letter "B." Do any children in the class have "B" names? Some children may enjoy pretending they have a new name. Invite them to choose their new names from the "B" list. "Today, we will all be 'B's!"

Props/Visual Aids
Use the name tags on page 12 to help everyone remember his or her new "B" name.

To Extend This Circle Time
Little Boy Blue's sheep and cows ran away while he was sleeping! Invite the children to act out the words to the song. One child can be Little Boy Blue and the other children may pretend to be animals. Have the children hide as Little Boy Blue "sleeps." Then Little Boy Blue awakens and blows a whistle to call the animals back. Let the children take turns playing Little Boy Blue.

Songs

"Baa, Baa, Black Sheep"
"B-I-N-G-O"
"Boom, Boom, Ain't It Great to Be Crazy?"
"Bow, Bow, Bow, Belinda"
"I'm Bringing Home a Baby Bumblebee"
"John Brown's Baby"
"Where Have You Been, Billy Boy?"

Snacks

bananas
biscuits
blackberries
blueberries
broccoli
brown bread
brownies
butter

10

Additional Activities

Bring out the **bubbles**! Make your own bubble solution by diluting liquid dish soap with water. Use a variety of items to make bubbles: straws, berry baskets, six-pack plastic rings and pipe cleaners bent to look like "b"s.

Invite the children to make their own **beanbags**. Provide a variety of dried beans and have the children scoop the beans into sturdy plastic bags that zip closed. Check to see that the bags are securely fastened (you may want to seal with duct tape). Enjoy playing beanbag toss games with buckets or taped areas on the floor for "targets."

Decorate an empty oatmeal box for a class **Button Box**. Ask the children to bring in buttons and use them for a variety of sorting activities. You can count how many buttons are certain colors or shapes and how many holes each button has. Supply small bowls or a clean egg carton for the sorting activities.

What is your favorite **book**? Invite the children to bring their favorite books to school to share with the class. Ask other adults in the school about their favorite books. What other people might the children ask about favorite books? Write letters to find out the mayor's favorite book or the TV weather reporter's favorite.

Bring in a variety of **balls**. Have the children experiment to see which balls are best for bouncing.

Books to Share

Degen, Bruce. *Jamberry*. HarperCollins Publishers, 1983. A rollicking rhyme about a boy and a bear who squires him through a fantastic world of berries. Exuberant, colorful illustrations.

Hale, Irene. *Brown Bear in a Brown Chair*. Atheneum, 1983. Brown Bear, the same color as his chair, is sat upon very often. Brown Bear's solution to his problem is told in a cumulative story, illustrated with brightly painted collages.

Little, Jean. *Bats About Baseball*. Viking, 1995. Ryder's grandmother is bats about baseball, and when the season starts it's hard to talk to her about anything else. During an exciting game, however, Ryder discovers that she really is listening.

Manushkin, Fran. *Buster Loves Buttons!* Harper & Row, 1985. After buying billions of buttons and filling button baskets, buckets, boxes, bottles and his bag, Buster begins stealing them from people's clothing. There a lots of "b"s in this humorous story with a happy ending.

McCloskey, Robert. *Blueberries for Sal*. Viking Press, 1948. Little Sal and Little Bear get mixed up among the blueberries on Blueberry Hill and almost end up with each other's mothers.

Reid, Margarette S. *The Button Box*. Dutton's Children's Books, 1990. A little boy loves to play with all the beautiful buttons in Grandma's button box.

West, Colin. *Buzz, Buzz, Buzz, Went Bumblebee*. Candlewick Press, 1996. Bumblebee buzzes around bothering everyone until he comes to gentle Butterfly who understands that busy Bee is just looking for a friend. Humorous watercolor and ink illustrations.

Tapes and CDs

McGrath, Bob. "Baa, Baa, Black Sheep" from *Sing Along with Bob, Vol. 1*. Kids' Records, 1984.

Rashad, Phylicia. "Little Boy Blue" from *Baby's Nursery Rhymes*. Lightyear Records, 1991.

Roth, Kevin. "Little Boy Blue" from *The Sandman: Lullabies and Night Time Songs*. Marlboro Records, 1988.

Various Performers. "Baby Bumblebee" and "Boom, Boom, Ain't It Great to Be Crazy?" from *Disney's Silly Songs*. Walt Disney Records, 1988.

 # My name is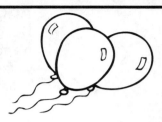

B

 # My name is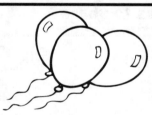

B

C

Who Stole the Cookie from the Cookie Jar?

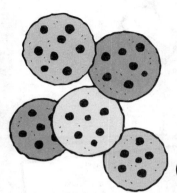

Cookies

Who stole the cookie from the cookie jar? (group)
(Name) stole the cookie from the cookie jar! (group)
Who me? (child)
Yes, you! (group)
Couldn't be! (child)
Then who? (group)
(New name) stole the cookie from the cookie jar! (group)

C

Talk About

This is a great call and response song! Once the children learn the pattern, they will sing the song endlessly, especially on a field trip bus! To help the children learn the call and response pattern, use the illustrations on page 16. Enlarge the pictures and use them on a chart or a flannel board or as cards to be passed from child to child within the group.

Props/Visual Aids

Bring in a large cookie jar. Place objects beginning with the letter "C" inside the jar. You might include a crayon, cup, cookie cutter, candy cane, cotton ball or pictures of "C" things (see page 17). Have the children take turns removing an item and naming it for the class. Invite them to bring additional "C" items from home to add to the jar.

To Extend This Circle Time

Make Crazy Cookies. Use the following recipe for simple sugar cookies or buy refrigerated tubes of prepared dough.

Callie's Old-Fashioned Sugar Cookies

1½ c. (360 ml) flour
½ tsp. (2.5 ml) baking powder
½ tsp. (2.5 ml) salt
½ tsp. (2.5 ml) soda
½ tsp. (2.5 ml) sugar

½ c. (120 ml) butter
1 egg
2 T. (30 ml) milk
1 tsp. (5 ml) vanilla

Sift together the first five dry ingredients. Cut in the softened butter. Blend in the egg, milk and vanilla. On a floured board, roll out to ¹⁄₁₆" (.16 cm) thick. Cut into desired shapes and bake at 400°F (204°C) for 6 to 8 minutes. This makes two dozen cookies.

To make your cookies "crazy," let the children choose from a variety of cookie cutters. After the baked cookies have cooled, have fun decorating them with colored frostings, sprinkles, chips, cereal pieces and candy. Allow the children to make their cookies as crazy as they want them to be!

 Songs

"Clap Your Hands"
"Clementine"
"Cobbler, Cobbler, Mend My Shoe"
"Comin' 'Round the Mountain"
"The Crawdad Song"
"Jimmy Crack Corn"
"Little Red Caboose"

 Snacks

cantaloupe
carrots
cookies
corn bread
cornflakes
cupcakes
crackers and cheese

Additional Activities

Place some "C" items in your sensory table. Try cornmeal with cups for pouring and measuring, or field corn, both on and off the cob.

Make **crumbs**. Put a variety of food in sealed plastic bags, such as cookies, crackers and cereal. Invite the children to break apart the food pieces to make crumbs. Use the crumbs as a topping for a yogurt, pudding or ice cream snack.

After you make crumbs, you may have to **clean**! Children enjoy cleaning, so plan a Class Cleanup Day. Make a list of things that can be safely cleaned by the children. You may wish to place these items on a drop cloth in one area of your room. Provide buckets, warm soapy water, sponges and brushes. Turn on some music and clean! You will want to inform parents of this activity so the children can dress appropriately.

Set up a **card** shop in your dramatic play area. Provide folded paper in several colors, markers, stickers and other art materials for the children to create their own cards. Use a shelf to display the cards.

Find "C" things to **count**. How many clouds can you see through the classroom window? Count the children in each carpool. How many cups do you need at snack time? Count the chairs in the room. How many crayons are in your box? Do any of the children have cats or chickens?

Books to Share

De Paola, Tomie. *Charlie Needs a Cloak*. Prentice Hall, 1973. Charlie the shepherd shears his sheep, cards and spins the wool, weaves and dyes the cloth, and sews a beautiful new red cloak.

Foreman, Michael. *Cat & Canary*. Dial Books for Young Readers, 1985. Beautiful paintings illustrate the story of a city cat who wishes to fly like his best friend Canary. And one day, he does.

Hersom, Kathleen, and Donald. *The Copycat*. Atheneum, 1989. This humorous rhyming story is about a cat who copies all the other animals from mooing at cows to croaking with frogs.

Himmelman, John. *The Clover County Carrot Contest*. Silver Press, 1991. Everyone in the Wright family competes in the Clover County Carrot Contest.

Moffatt, Judith. *Who Stole the Cookies?* Grosset & Dunlap, 1996. Cut-paper illustrations and rhyming text tell about each in a series of animals who deny taking the cookies but help to track a trail of crumbs to the cave of a cookie-loving bear.

Pryor, Ainslie. *The Baby Blue Cat and the Whole Batch of Cookies*. Viking Kestrel, 1989. Mama Cat's babies all have favorite treats, cupcakes, strawberries and cream, and especially cookies! When Mama Cat bakes cookies for them, Baby Blue Cat can't resist a taste or two too many.

Wellington, Monica. *Mr. Cookie Baker*. Dutton's Children's Books, 1992. Mr. Baker mixes his cookie dough, cuts out shapes with cookie cutters, decorates them with colored sprinkles and waits for his shop to be crowded with customers. Bright stylized paintings illustrate the text.

Tapes and CDs

Beall, Pamela Conn, and Susan Hagen Nipp. "Little Red Caboose" from *Wee Sing Fun 'n' Folk*. Price Stern Sloan, 1989.

Merrill Staton Children's Voices. "Clap Your Hands" from *Music 1 . . . 2 . . . 3, Vol. 1: Counting and Action Songs*. Columbia Special Products, 1977.

Rashad, Phylicia. "Cobbler, Cobbler" from *Baby's Nursery Rhymes*. Lightyear Records, 1991.

Roth, Kevin. "She'll Be Coming 'Round the Mountain" from *Travel Song Sing Alongs*. Marlboro Records, 1994.

D

Braille ●●
●●

Hey, Diddle, Diddle

Hey, diddle, diddle
The cat and the fiddle
The cow jumped over the moon.
The little dog laughed to see such sport
And the dish ran away with the spoon.

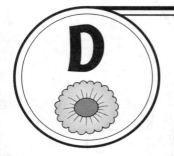

Talk About

With the children's help, make a list of words that begin with the letter "D." Use the list to write a new version of the nursery rhyme, substituting the new "D" words for the nouns and verbs. The children will enjoy the silly images in their new rhymes! For example:

Hey, diddle, diddle
The dinosaur on the drum
The doll danced over the daisies.
The little dog discoed to see such delight
And the dish ran away with the duck.

Props/Visual Aids

Use the clip art on page 20 as prompts for your new version of the rhyme. The children may also enjoy cutting "D" pictures from magazines or drawing their own.

To Extend This Circle Time

The words *Hey, diddle, diddle* are nonsense words; they have no meaning but make the rhyme more fun. Invite the children to suggest other nonsense phrases to make class time routines more fun. For example: Dicky-doo drop, time to stop; Rinkety dinkety doo doo doo, let's line up two by two.

Songs
"Dance to Your Daddy"
"Day-O (The Banana Boat Song)"
"Diddle, Diddle, Dumpling, My Son John"
"Dinga Dinga Doodle"
"Down by the Bay"
"Little White Duck"

Snacks
dip (with assorted raw vegetables for dipping)
dinosaur-shaped graham crackers
doughnuts
dried fruit (including dates)

Additional Activities

Set aside an area of the classroom for displaying plastic **dinosaurs**. Be sure to label any animals the children bring from home. Do any of the dinosaur names begin with "D" such as *diplodocus* or *dimetrodon*?

Stop at a flower shop and purchase some **daisies**, **daffodils** or **day lilies** for your classroom. Use **dandelions** for paintbrushes in your art center.

Borrow a food dehydrator and **dry** some fruit for a snack.

Invite a **dentist** to visit your classroom or take a field trip to a nearby dental clinic. What are some of the instruments a dentist uses? Invite the children to share stories about their visits to the dentist.

Dance! Children love to move to music, and dancing is the perfect way to work out some wiggles before a quiet activity. Share some simple dance steps with the children such as the box step or waltz. Introduce a variety of music as well, both slow and fast, such as country, pop or classical. Invite the children to move in rhythm with the beat.

Books to Share

Crebbin, June. *Danny's Duck.* Candlewick Press, 1995. Danny visits a mother duck near his school daily, one day her nest is empty and she is gone. Then Danny and his teacher make a wonderful discovery. Illustrated with warm and realistic watercolor paintings.

Hooks, William H. *A Dozen Dizzy Dogs.* Bantam Books, 1990. A dozen dizzy dogs with spots, stripes and funny hats dig up a bone and share some adventures.

Janovitz, Marilyn. *Hey, Diddle, Diddle.* Hyperion Books for Children, 1992. Illustrated with water-color and colored pencil, this book is a cheerful adaptation of the familiar nursery rhyme.

Otto, Carolyn. *Ducks, Ducks, Ducks.* HarperCollins Publishers, 1991. This story follows four country ducks to town and its rhythmic text contains many "D"s. Bath time is described as "dipping ducks, dripping ducks, dunking, ducking, duckling ducks." Watercolor and pencil illustrations.

Strickland, Paul, and Henrietta. *Dinosaur Roar!* Dutton's Children's Books, 1994. Humorous, colorful illustrations and rhyming text present all kinds of dinosaurs.

Svatos, Ladislav. *Dandelion.* Doubleday & Company, Inc., 1976. A simple but poetic story of the life cycle of the dandelion with clear and detailed drawings.

Tapes and CDs

Kallick, Kathy. "Hey, Diddle, Diddle" from *What Do You Dream About?* Kaleidoscope Records, Inc., 1990.

Raven, Nancy. "Hey, Diddle, Diddle" from *Thoroughly Modern Mother Goose.* Pacific Cascade Records, 1977.

Roth, Kevin. "Down by the Bay" from *Dinosaurs, Dragons & Other Children's Songs.* Marlboro Records, Inc., 1990.

Various Performers. "Dance to Your Daddy" from *Golden Slumbers.* Caedmon, 1988.

20

E

Braille

The Elephant Song

One elephant went out to play
On a spider's web one day.
He had such enormous fun
That he called for another elephant to come.
"HEY, ELEPHANT!"

Talk About

Enormous is a great "E" word! With the children, make a list of things that are enormous. Keep in mind that what may *seem* enormous to a preschool child may not be enormous to you. Invite the children to pretend that they are enormous. Then pretend that everything else is enormous, and they are very, very small. Write a class story about something that was enormous fun, using as many "E" words as possible. "One *evening* we went to the zoo and saw that *every* elephant was very *excited*. *Each* elephant ate *eighteen* egg salad sandwiches."

Props/Visual Aids

Use the enormous elephant on page 23 when writing your class story. Bind the pages together to make an enormous book.

To Extend This Circle Time

Provide large grocery bags, paper towel or wrapping paper tubes, scissors, glue or stapler and gray paint. Cut headbands from the grocery bags to fit the children. Have each child cut a large pair of ears (pattern on page 24) from a bag and paint them gray. Then paint a paper towel tube gray and allow the paint to dry. Attach the ears to the headband and hold the tube for an elephant nose. Play some appropriate music (marches with lots of tuba would work well) and join the children in an "enormous elephant dance."

"Eensy Weensy Spider"
"Eeny, Meany, Miney, Moe"
"Engine, Engine, Number Nine"

egg rolls
egg salad
other foods made with egg
elephant ear pastries
enchiladas
English muffins

Additional Activities

Place clean **eggshells** in the sensory table for the children to break. You may want to dye the shells first, so the children may mix colors as they crush the pieces.

Provide a variety of clip-on earrings in your dramatic play area.

Supply magazine pictures of different animals. Invite the children to make an "**ear**" collage with the pictures. Can they tell from what animal the different kinds of ears came? Which animal has the biggest ears? The longest?

Earth, **environment** and **ecology** are all very important "E" words. Spend time learning about ecology with your children. What are some things your class can do to help the environment and make the Earth a healthier place? You might have a playground cleanup day or place a container for recycling paper in your classroom. What are things children can do at home? Make a class **exhibit** of ideas.

Create a menu of **entrees** for a restaurant in the dramatic play area. The children can use pretend food to create meals and serve them to customers.

Books to Share

Auch, Mary Jane. *The Easter Egg Farm*. Holiday House, 1992. Pauline the hen lays very unusual eggs, but she and her owner think they are beautiful, and together they open an Easter egg farm. Humorous, colorful illustrations are integral to the story.

McGovern, Ann. *Eggs on Your Nose*. Macmillan Publishing Company, 1977. This humorous story told in rhyme has "eggs everywhere!" as a little boy begins to eat eggs by himself for the first time.

Paxton, Tom. *Englebert the Elephant*. Morrow Junior Books, 1990. Englebert the elephant is invited to a royal ball! This rhyming story tells how his dancing skills and good manners surprise everyone there.

Stevenson, James. *The Great Big Especially Beautiful Easter Egg*. Greenwillow Books, 1983. At Easter, Grandpa tells his two grandchildren about his long-ago search for an enormous Easter egg to give to his friend Charlotte. Cartoon-like drawings illustrate the tale.

Tapes and CDs

Beall, Pamela Conn, and Susan Hagen Nipp. "The Eensy Weensy Spider" from *Wee Sing Children's Songs and Fingerplays*. Price Stern Sloan, 1990.

McGrath, Bob, and Katharine Smithrim. "Engine, Engine" from *Songs & Games for Toddlers*. Kids' Records, 1985.

Paxton, Tom. "Englebert the Elephant" from *Marvelous Toy*. PAX Records, 1984, 1991.

Sharon, Lois, and Bram. "Eensy Weensy Spider" and "One Elephant" from *Great Big Hits*. A & M Records, Inc., 1992.

Sharon, Lois, and Bram. "One Elephant Went out to Play" from *Sharon, Lois & Bram's Elephant Show Record*. Elephant Records/A & M Records, 1986.

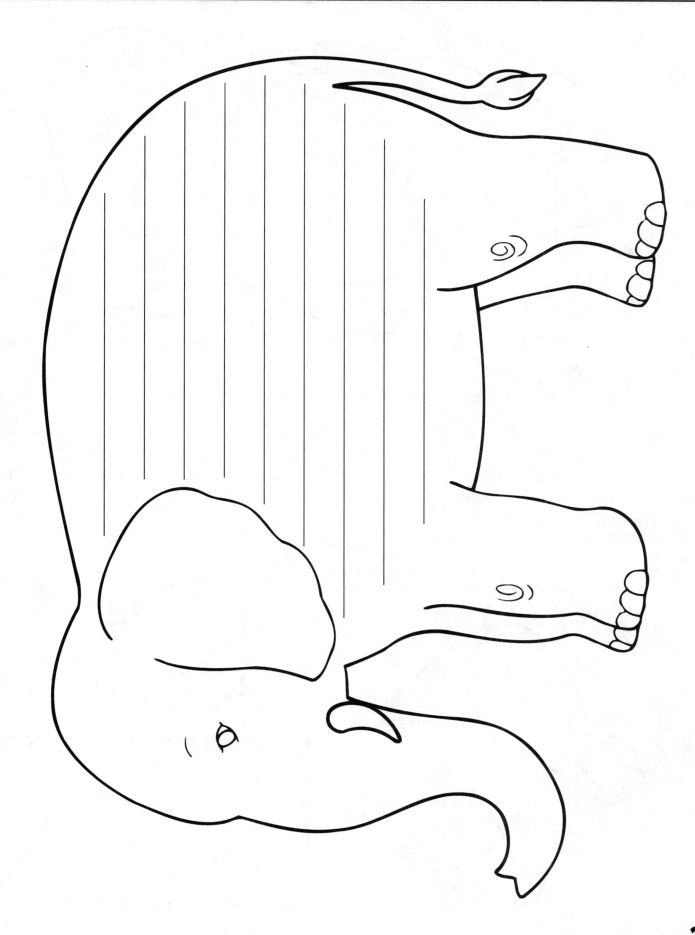

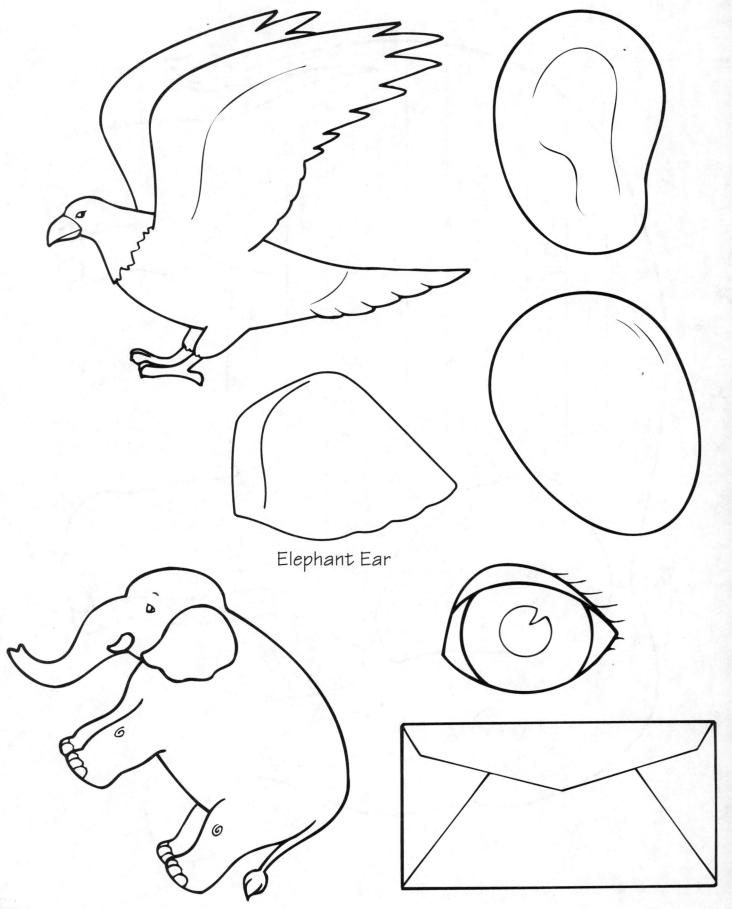

Elephant Ear

F

International Morse Code

Braille

The Farmer in the Dell

The farmer in the dell, the farmer in the dell,
Hi-ho the derry-o, the farmer in the dell.

Verses:

The farmer takes a wife	The dog takes a cat
The wife takes a child	The cat takes a rat
The child takes a nurse	The rat takes the cheese
The nurse takes a dog	The cheese stands alone

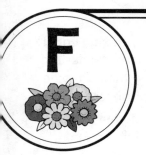

Talk About

Play the familiar game with your children. Have all the children join hands and walk in a circle with one child, the "farmer" in the center. The "farmer" chooses a "wife" to come to the center of the ring, the "wife" chooses a "child" and so on for each verse. The children inside the ring may join hands and walk in the opposite direction to create their own circle. When the "cheese" is chosen, all the children join hands in the outer circle and the "cheese" becomes the "farmer" to play the game again.

The farmer had many people (and animals) in his family. Send home the family tree on page 27 for the children to complete with their families. Remember, many of your children may come from nontraditional family groups. Sing the songs and play the game using the names of children's family members. You might sing, "Jimmy's in the dell . . . Jimmy has a mom." You can also sing using the names of friends: "Chang is my friend . . . "

Props/Visual Aids

Cut a large "F" from tagboard. Ask the children to bring in a recent photograph or take new pictures in class. Attach the pictures to the "F" and display it on a bulletin board with the title "We Are All Friends" or "Join Our Family."

To Extend This Circle Time

Many of the children may not live close to their extended families. Some families have friends or neighbors that fill in for traditional family roles. Use the activity on page 28 to develop circles of family or friends for the children. Make a copy for each child, and place his or her photograph in the center circle. Invite the child to add photographs or draw pictures of friends or family in the outer circles. Some of the families in your class may be connected!

Songs

"Fish and Chips and Vinegar"
"Five Green and Speckled Frogs"
"Fooba Wooba John"
"Frere Jacques"
"Put Your Finger in the Air"

Snacks

fajitas
finger foods
fish sticks
French fries
French toast
fruit

Additional Activities

Put craft **feathers** in your sensory table or a plastic tub. Do not use feathers you may have found outside since they may harbor mites. Show the children how to gently brush down their arms with the feathers or how to gently tickle a friend's face. Sort the feathers by color or length. Do two feathers tickle more than one feather?

Use the craft feathers as brushes in a painting project. Pour small amounts of tempera paint mixed with a little liquid dish soap on paper plates. Dip the feathers in the paint and gently brush on paper. Gentle strokes combined with small amounts of paint will allow the children to see the delicate lines the feather can make.

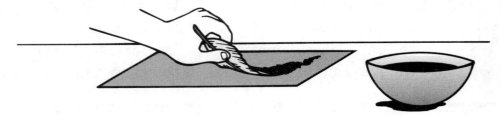

Finger paint! Use commercially available paint or make your own by mixing equal parts of liquid starch and soap flakes. Add powdered tempera to achieve the desired color. Add more starch if the paint is too thick and more soap if it is too thin. Provide rubber gloves for children who dislike the sensation of the paint on their fingers.

Visit a local **fire** station and talk to the firefighters, or invite one to visit your classroom. Make a group chart of fire safety rules. Demonstrate for the children and have them practice "stop, drop and roll" and "crawl low in smoke."

Use washable ink pads to make **fingerprints**. Use markers to add details to the fingerprints to make a variety of creatures. See Ed Emberley's *The Great Thumbprint Book*, Little, Brown and Company, 1977, for many creative ideas.

Books to Share

Adams, Georgie. *Fish Fish Fish*. Dial Books for Young Readers, 1993. Colorful collage illustrations introduce fascinating fish in all shapes, sizes and temperaments.

Carlstrom, Nancy White. *Fish and Flamingo*. Little, Brown and Company, 1993. Fish and flamingo are unlikely friends, but they share stories of their lives and special good-bye gifts. Luminous, jewel-toned oil paintings add richness to the story.

Parkinson, Kathy. *The Farmer in the Dell*. Albert Whitman & Company, 1988. Humorous illustrations give interesting details to the familiar nursery rhyme.

Priceman, Marjorie. *Friend or Frog?* Houghton Mifflin Company, 1989. When Kate must find a new home for her best friend Hilton the frog, she meets some interesting people. Humorous watercolor and ink illustrations.

Rae, Mary Maki. *The Farmer in the Dell, a Singing Game*. Viking Kestrel, 1988. Rich, folk art style paintings illustrate this version of the nursery rhyme. Music and directions for the circle dance game are included.

Wu, Norbert. *Fish Faces*. Henry Holt and Company, 1993. Stunning photographs capture in vivid detail many friendly and fierce, sad and mad, fish faces.

Tapes and CDs

Glazer, Tom. "Farmer in the Dell" from *Tom Glazer Sings Winnie the Pooh and Mother Goose*. Gateway Records/RTV Communications Group, Inc., 1991.

Greg and Steve. "Put Your Finger in the Air" from *Playing Favorites*. Youngheart Records, 1991.

McGrath, Bob. "Farmer in the Dell" from *Sing Along with Bob McGrath, Vol. 1*. Kids' Records, 1984.

Raffi. "Five Little Frogs" from *The Singable Songs Collection*. Shoreline/A & M Records, 1988.

My Family Tree

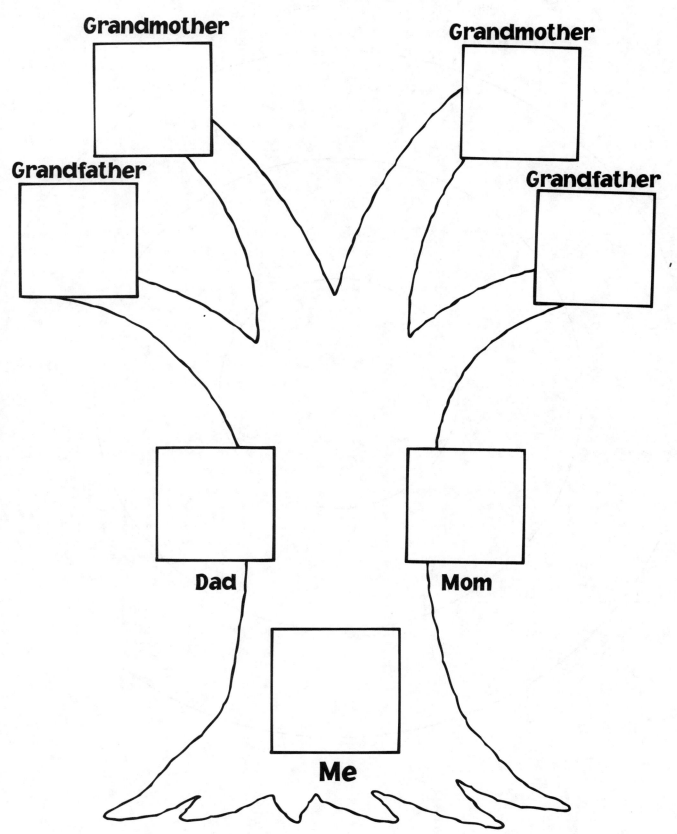

Grandmother

Grandmother

Grandfather

Grandfather

Dad

Mom

Me

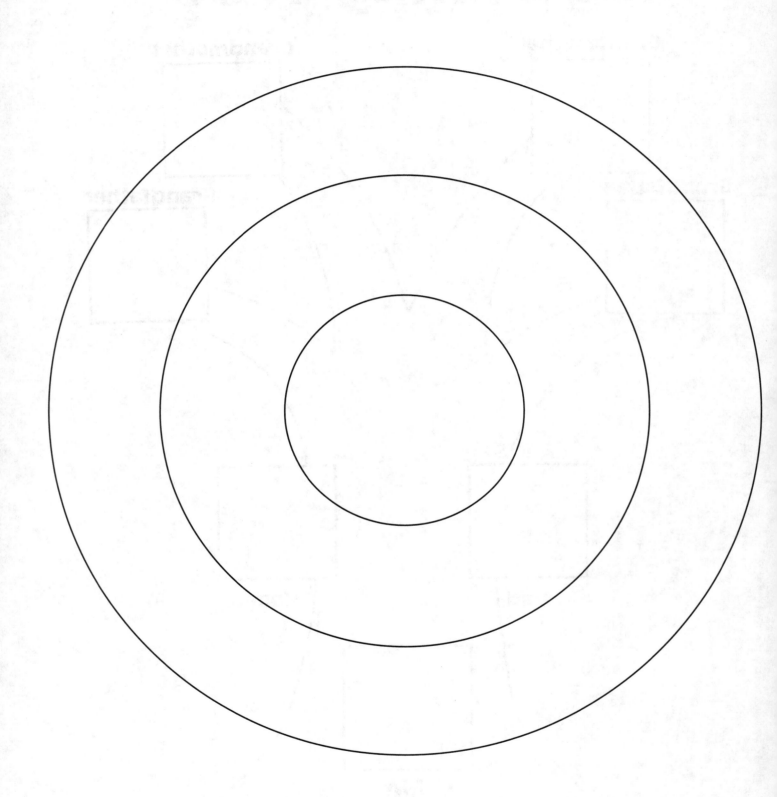

G

International Morse Code

Braille

The Green Grass Grew All Around

There was a tree out in the wood
The prettiest tree that you ever did see
Refrain
A tree in the wood and the green grass grew all around, all around
And the green grass grew all around
Verse 2
And on that tree there was a trunk
The prettiest trunk that you ever did see
Refrain
Trunk on the tree and the tree in the wood
And the green grass grew all around, all around
And the green grass grew all around
Additional verses also sung in reverse order for refrain.
And on that trunk there was a branch . . .
And on that branch there was a nest . . .
And in that nest there was an egg . . .
And in that egg there was a bird . . .
And on that bird there was a feather . . .

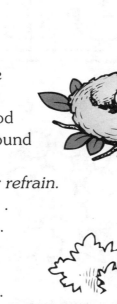

Talk About
This is a cumulative song, repeating each verse and ending with a common refrain. Use the picture cards on page 32 as visual prompts when you sing the song. Invite the children to add to or change the verses in the song and draw simple illustrations to accompany their ideas.

Props/Visual Aids
Enlarge the illustrations on page 32 to make a big book. Have the children color the pages and fasten them together. Write the lyrics for each illustration on the page and help the children identify all of the letter "G"s.

To Extend This Circle Time
Provide soil, cardboard egg cartons or small paper cups and grass seed. Have each child spoon soil into a container and sprinkle grass seed on top. Water and place the cups in a sunny window. In a few days the grass seed will sprout and grow. Create a simple graph to record how fast your grass grows.

songs

"Down on Grandpa's Farm"
"Go Tell Aunt Rhody (the Old Gray
    Goose Is Dead)"
"Going to the Zoo"
"Goosey, Goosey, Gander"

snacks

gingerbread
graham crackers
granola cereal or bars
grapefruit
grapes
guacamole

Additional Activities

Place **grass** seed in your sensory table. Be aware of children who may have allergies. Provide funnels, spoons and cups for pouring and measuring.

Invite the children to bring in different varieties and flavors of chewing **gum**. You may wish to discuss good chewing and disposal etiquette and then conduct a taste test. Which kinds of gum taste the best, last the longest or blow the best bubbles?

Divide the class into **groups** of two or three children. You might group them by colors of their clothing, types of shoes or other visual cues. See if they can guess on what the groups are based.

Cut out letter "G"s for the children to cover with **glue** and **glitter**.

Celebrate **grandparents**! Plan a special time for grandparents to visit your classroom. Help the children make invitations, prepare a special snack and simple program. You might include some songs and a sample of activities. Some children may not live near their grandparents or have relationships with them. Be sure to be sensitive to special situations and encourage these children to invite another special adult.

Books to Share

Asch, Frank. *MacGoose's Grocery*. Dial Press, 1978. Tired of waiting for customers in their grocery store, the MacGoose family goes for a walk, leaving the new egg to look after itself.

Balian, Lorna. *A Garden for a Groundhog*. Abingdon Press, 1985. Humorous illustrations help tell the story of Mr. and Mrs. O'Leary's plan to keep their groundhog from eating all the vegetables in the garden.

Bender, Robert. *The Three Billy Goats Gruff*. Henry Holt and Company, 1993. This familiar folktale with bold, colorful illustrations uses many "G"s. The goats graze on grass, and the troll tries to gobble and fill his gullet with goat!

Hines, Anna Grossnickle. *Grandma Gets Grumpy*. Clarion Books, 1988. When Lassen and her four cousins spend the night at Grandma's, they have fun but discover even Grandma has limits to her patience.

Moore, Elaine. *Grandma's Garden*. Lothrop, Lee & Shepard Books, 1994. Kim visits Grandma in the spring, when they fly a kite, huddle through a thunderstorm and sow seeds to begin the miracle of Grandma's garden.

Stevens, Janet. *The Three Billy Goats Gruff*. Harcourt Brace Jovanovich, 1987. The three Billy Goats Gruff, hungry for green grass, must outwit the troll to cross the bridge. This version is illustrated with watercolor and pencil.

Tapes and CDs

Roth, Kevin. "Green Grass Grew All Around" from *Oscar, Bingo and Buddies*. CMS Records, Inc., 1986.

Seeger, Pete. "Green Grass Grew All Around" from *Stories & Songs for Little Children*. High Windy Audio, 1989.

Sharon, Lois, and Bram. "Down on Grandpa's Farm" from *Great Big Hits*. Elephant Records, 1992.

Various Performers. "Going to the Zoo" from *Car Songs: Songs to Sing Anywhere*. Kimbo, 1990.

Gum

H

● ● ● ●
International Morse Code

Braille

Hello Song

To the tune of "Row, Row, Row Your Boat"
Hello, hello, hello to you
How are you today?
I'm glad that you are here with us,
Let's have some fun and play!

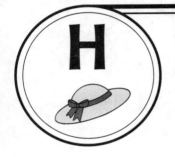

Kon'nichi wa!

Talk About

There are many different "hello" songs. Use the one above, sing one you already know or make up a new song with your children. Have the children take turns being the classroom "hello" person and greeting everyone who comes to your room. Use your hello song to help the children greet each other individually and learn everyone's names. For example: "Hello, hello, hello to Sam . . . "

Props/Visual Aids

Teach the children how to say "hello" or "good day" in other languages. Reproduce the chart on page 36. Teach one of the new words in the "Hello Song" every week. French: Bonjour! (bon jhoor). Norwegian: Hallo! (HA-lO). Spanish: ¡Hola! (O la). Italian: Buno giorno! (bwohn JOR-no). Russian: Zdravstvuite! (ZDRAHST-voo-ee-tyee). German: Guten Tag or hallo! (goo-ten TAHK). Japanese: kon'nichi wa! (koan-nee-chee-wa). Hebrew: Shalom. (sha lōm).

To Extend This Circle Time

Start a Hello Club to greet new students in your class or school. Invite the class to help you list things a new child would need to learn. Your list might include: where the bathrooms are, where the playground balls are kept, how the class lines up to go outside or where the children's mailboxes or cubbies are located. Assign a buddy from the Hello Club to be with the new child during his or her first week of school.

Songs

"Ha, Ha, This A-Way"
"Hokey Pokey"
"Home on the Range"
"Humpty Dumpty"
"If You're Happy and You Know It"

Snacks

doughnut holes
ham
hamburgers
hominy
honey
honeycomb-shaped cerea
hot dogs

34

Additional Activities

Ask a parent who works in an office or contact a print shop to save paper **hole** punches for you to use in your sensory table. You may also use the hole punches in a variety of art projects.

Hearts are not just for Valentine's Day! Use heart-shaped cookie cutters with playdough, heart-shaped sponges for painting and colorful construction paper hearts and heart stickers for collages.

Teach the children the actions for the "**Hokey Pokey**" and perform it for parents or another class.

Make newspaper **hats**. Unfold three or four sheets of newspaper and place on top of a child's head. Have another adult help you use long strips of masking tape to shape the newspaper around the top of the child's head to form the hat's crown.
Roll the edges of the newspaper up to form the brim of the hat and secure it with more tape. Allow the children to decorate their hats with paint, tissue paper, hole punches, feathers or other art materials. Place a variety of hats in your dramatic play area.

Staying **healthy** is important! It can also be difficult to do in a large group of children. Good **hygiene** can reduce the number of children's illnesses in a group setting. One of the best ways to reduce the spread of germs is through good and frequent **hand washing**. Demonstrate good hand washing technique and practice with the children. Post copies of the hand washing chart on page 37 near the classroom sink and in the bathrooms. Make a copy to send home with each child.

Books to Share

Fowler, Allan. *Horses, Horses, Horses*. Children's Press, 1992. Clear photographs and simple text describe horses, their beauty and usefulness.

Fregosi, Claudia. *The Happy Horse*. Greenwillow Books, 1977. This simple story follows a happy horse through his day from sun up to star shine.

Martin, Bill Jr. *The Happy Hippopotami*. Harcourt Brace Jovanovich, 1991. Happy hippopotamuses climb aboard the picnic buses for a hippo holiday in the merry month of May. Whimsical pastel paintings illustrate this rhyming story.

Milstein, Linda. *Amanda's Perfect Hair*. Tambourine Books, 1993. With all the hoopla about Amanda's long, thick, beautiful hair, people hardly notice Amanda. So she devices a hair-raising plan to show how special she really is. Bright, cartoon-like illustrations.

Smith, William Jay. *Ho for a Hat!* Little, Brown and Company, 1989. This is a delightful, rhythmic celebration of hats: hats made of velvet, hats made of silk, hats like plates or bottles of milk. Humorous illustrations depict children and animals wearing every possible kind of hat.

Waddell, Martin. *The Happy Hedgehog Band*. Candlewick Press, 1991. Harry is a happy hedgehog who loves noise so much, he forms a band which starts all the woods humming. Wonderfully animated illustrations bring the band to life.

Tapes and CDs

Barolk Folk with Madeline MacNeil, and Barbara Hess. "Humpty Dumpty" from *Girls and Boys, Come out to Play*. Music for Little People, 1991.

Bartels, Joanie. "Hokey Pokey" from *Dancin' Magic*. Discovery Music, 1991.

McGrath, Bob. "Ha, Ha, This A-Way" from *Sing Along with Bob, Vol. 2*. Kids' Records, 1985.

Various Performers. "If You're Happy and You Know It" from *Kiddin' Around*. Music for Little People, 1991.

"Hello" Chart

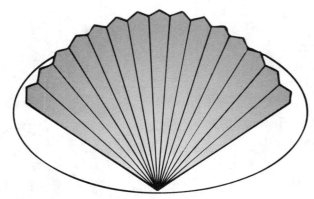

Japanese: Kon'nichi wa

German: Guten Tag

Norwegian: Hallo

Hebrew: Shalom

Russian: Zdravstvuite

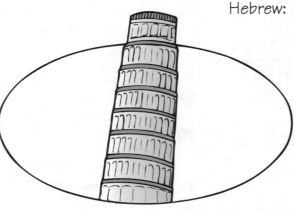

Italian: Buno Giorno

French: Bonjour

Spanish: Hola

36

Hand Washing Chart

Lather.

Rinse.

Repeat.

I

We Like Ice Cream

To the tune of "Are You Sleeping?"
We like ice cream; we like ice cream.
Yes, we do! Yes, we do!
(Child's name) likes vanilla; (Child's name) like vanilla.
We do, too! We do, too!

Talk About

Sing the song using the names of the children in your room and substituting their favorite ice cream flavors. Make a graph of the children's favorite flavors. You may also want to survey other classes. What is your school's favorite flavor? Do the teachers like different flavors than the children? Extend the activity by asking how the children like to eat ice cream: in a cone, sundae, shake or by the spoonful.

Props/Visual Aids

Use the patterns of ice cream scoops and cones on page 41 to create your graph. Invite each child to color a scoop of ice cream to represent his or her favorite flavor and stack the scoops on the cones, one for each flavor. Which ice cream cone is the tallest?

To Extend This Circle Time

Borrow an ice cream maker and follow the recipe and manufacturer's directions to make ice cream with your children. Many ice cream recipes use raw eggs; be sure to use pasteurized eggs in any recipe calling for uncooked eggs. If an ice cream maker is not available, you might use the following to make a frozen treat with your children.

Take a field trip to visit a local ice cream parlor. You may be able to observe how ice cream is made or how the ingredients differ in various flavors.

Set up an ice cream parlor in your dramatic play area. Empty ice cream buckets, bowls, empty bottles of toppings, scoops and spoons may all serve as props.

Invite parents for an Ice Cream Social Open House. After some family time in your classroom, provide the guests and children with several flavors of ice cream and toppings, and enjoy the treats you make together!

Cranberry-Orange Ice

2 c. (480 ml) sugar   2 c. (480 ml) orange juice
4 c. (960 ml) cranberry juice cocktail

In a medium saucepan, combine the sugar and orange juice. Stir over medium heat until the sugar dissolves. Cool to room temperature. Stir in cranberry juice cocktail. Pour into a 9" (23 cm) square pan. Cover with foil or plastic wrap and place in freezer until firm, three to six hours. Scrape frozen mixture with a fork until pieces resemble finely crushed ice. Serve immediately.

Recipe adapted from Ice Cream *by Mable and Gar Hoffman, H.P. Books, 1981.*

"Goodnight, Irene"
"Inchworm"
"Inka Dinka Doo"
"Itsy Bitsy Spider"

flavored ice (snow cones)
ice cream
Italian salad dressing for dipping raw
   vegetables

Additional Activities

Paint with colored **ice** cubes. Thin several colors of tempera paint with water and use the diluted paint to fill an old ice cube tray. When the ice cubes are almost frozen, inset a craft stick or plastic spoon in each cube. Remove the cubes when they are completely frozen and invite the children to paint with them.

Use food coloring to make colored ice cubes for your sensory table. Put warm water in the table and release the colored cubes. Ask the children to observe what happens. Provide scoops, funnels, cups and other water toys for the children to use.

How many **inches** is it? Make copies of the clip art inch on page 42 or provide rulers with the inches clearly marked. Invite the children to work with a partner to answer questions such as "How many inches is your foot?" Your thumb? How many inches is your pencil? How many inches wide is the classroom door?"

An **iguana** can be an interesting classroom visitor. Check with the families in your class to see if any have a pet iguana. What does the iguana eat? What does it like to do?

An **illustrator** is someone who draws pictures for books. Bring a collection of books illustrated by the same person to share with the class. Help the children identify the similarities in style, color, technique or medium used in the books. Invite the children to illustrate a story they have written or another familiar story.

Books to Share

Caseley, Judith. *Mr. Green Peas*. Greenwillow Books, 1995. Norman is sad because he is the only one in his nursery school class without a pet, until he gets an outrageous iguana!

Greene, Carol. *Ice Is . . . Whee!* Children's Press, 1983. Two children discover many of the things ice is: cold, slippery, wet and fun! Illustrated with bright cartoon-like drawings.

Hertz, Ole. *Tobias Goes Ice Fishing*. Carolrhoda Books, 1984. In Greenland winter, Tobias and his father fish through the ice that covers the fjord. Simple line drawings and watercolors illustrate the story.

Rey, Margaret, and Allan J. Shalleck. *Curious George Goes to an Ice Cream Shop*. Houghton Mifflin Company, 1989. There are so many colorful, delicious flavors of ice cream in Mr. Herb's store, Curious George doesn't know which to try first. Of course, it doesn't take long for him to make a mess, but he turns the trouble into triumph.

Tapes and CDs

Bethie. "Itty Bitty Inchworm" and "Ivana the Iguana" from *Bethie's Really Silly Songs About Animals*. Discovery Music, 1993.

Monet, Lisa. "Itsy Bitsy Spider" from *Circle Time: Songs and Rhymes for the Very Young*. Monet Productions, 1986.

Murray, Anne. "Inchworm" from *There's a Hippo in My Tub*. Capitol, 1979.

Paper Bag Players. "Ice Cream Cone" from *Music for 4's, 5's and 6's*. CMS Records, Inc., 1981.

Various Performers. "Itsy Bitsy Spider" from *For Our Children*. Walt Disney Records, 1991.

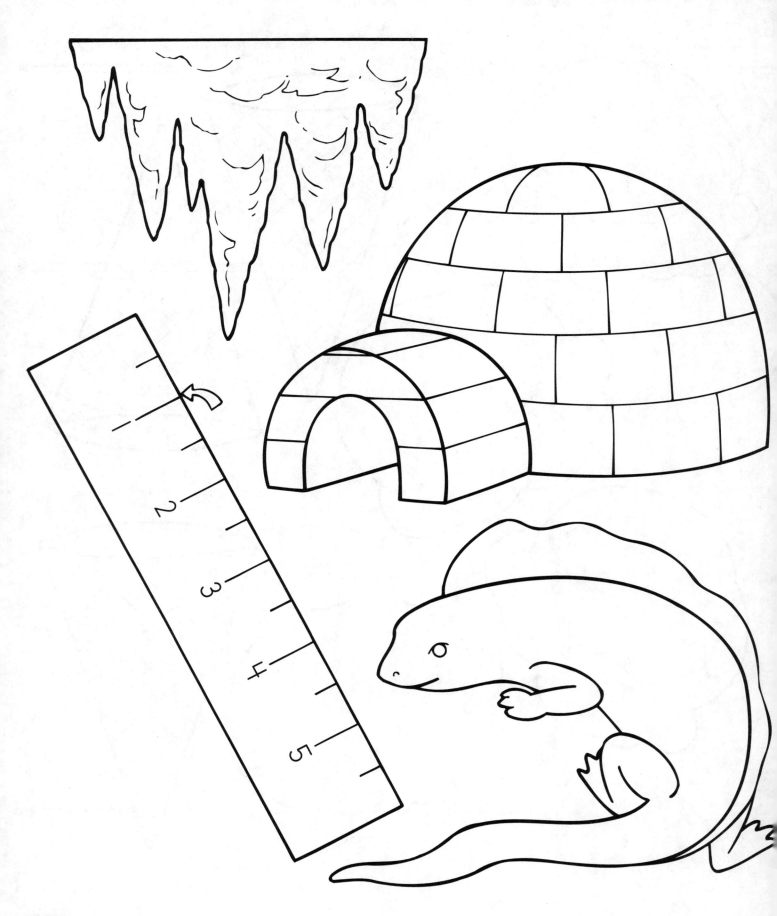

J

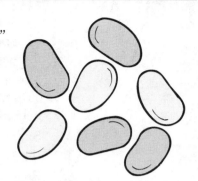
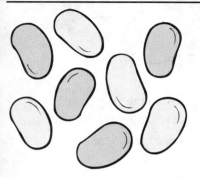

Jelly Beans

To the tune of "Twinkle, Twinkle, Little Star"
Jelly beans are fun to eat.
They are such a silly treat.
Green and orange and red and blue
Sometimes they are hard to chew.
Jelly beans are fun to eat.
I think they are my favorite treat!

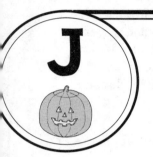

Talk About
Bring a basket of jelly beans to circle time, enough for each child to have one. (Be sure to explain that these jelly beans are not for eating, but you have set some aside for a treat later.) Pass the basket around the circle, so each child may choose a jelly bean. Invite each child to examine his or her jelly bean carefully. What color is it? Does it have a smell? Are there any marks on it? Could he or she find it again if all the jelly beans were put back in the basket? Use the jelly beans to measure different objects in the classroom. A pencil is seven jelly beans long. How many jelly beans long is a shoe?

Props/Visual Aids
Use the patterns on page 45 to create some jelly bean sorting activities. Write the numerals 1 to 5 on the baskets and invite the children to place the correct number of paper (or real) jelly beans on each basket. Another set of jelly beans could be sorted by color into the same colors of baskets.

To Extend This Circle Time
Have a jumping jelly bean relay. Divide the children into three groups and place them around your open area. Give the first child in one group a "jumping jelly bean." That child jumps to the next group and hands the jelly bean to the first child and then goes to the end to that group's line. The child with the bean jumps to the third group and again hands off the bean. Continue until everyone has had a turn to jump. End the game with a jumping jelly bean parade to your snack area and serve some jelly bean treats for everyone.

"Jack and Jill"
"Jack Be Nimble"
"Jim Along Josie"
"John Jacob Jingleheimer Schmidt"
"Rig a Jig Jig"

beef jerky
jam or jelly on crackers
Jell-O™
jelly beans

Additional Activities

Finger-paint with **Jell-O™**. Follow the package directions to make a quick set. When the gelatin is a soft gel, spoon a small amount on several trays. Children can use their fingers or a sponge brush to create designs. When each design is finished, place a piece of paper on the gelatin to transfer the image. Remove the paper and allow the print to dry.

Measure how far the children can **jump**. Place a strip of masking tape on the floor and invite each child to jump from a standing position behind the tape. If the weather allows, try this activity outside in a sandy area.

Sing the "**Jelly Beans**" song or other "J" songs while the children play jingle bells in rhythm with the song's beat.

Preschool children are just beginning to understand and appreciate **jokes**. Share some simple jokes with the children and invite them to tell jokes they have heard. Be prepared for some nonsensical fun! Knock-knock jokes are especially popular, in part because of the consistently repeated phrases. Here is one to share; you may wish to check with your library for children's joke books. "Knock-knock." "Who's there?" "Banana." "Banana who?" "Knock-knock." "Who's there?" "Banana." "Banana who?" "Knock-knock." "Who's there?" "Orange." "Orange who?" " 'Orange' you glad I didn't say *banana* again?"

Bring in simple **jigsaw** puzzles for the children to complete. As the year progresses and the children become more skillful, the puzzles can become more complex.

Books to Share

Cole, Joanna. *Norma Jean, Jumping Bean.* Random House, 1987. Norma Jean, whose love for jumping is a bit excessive, unhappily stops when her friends complain, but finally finds a time and place for jumping.

Duncan, Alice Faye. *Willie Jerome.* Macmillan Books for Young Readers, 1995. Nobody appreciates Willie Jerome's jazz trumpet playing except his sister Judy, who finally makes Mama listen to the music speak.

Kite, Patricia. *Down in the Sea: The Jellyfish.* Albert Whitman & Company, 1993. Brilliant photographs illustrate this introduction to the jiggly jellyfish. Simple text describes its physical characteristics, life cycle and eating habits.

Miller, Edna. *Jumping Bean.* Prentice-Hall, Inc., 1979. Many small animals wonder at the little bean that jumps, but in time, its mystery is revealed. Soft detailed watercolors illustrate the jumping bean's story.

Peters, Lisa Westberg. *Purple Delicious Blackberry Jam.* Arcade Publishing, 1992. When Freddy and Muff persuade Grandma to make blackberry jam, the three set off on a juicy, prickly, messy, bubbly adventure.

Royston, Angela. *Jungle Animals.* Simon & Schuster, 1991. Clear photographs and simple text introduce eight jungle animals: monkey, jaguar, tree frog, crocodile, orangutan, toucan, iguana and sloth.

Tapes and CDs

McGrath, Bob. "Rig a Jig Jig" from *Sing Along with Bob, Vol. 2.* Kids' Records, 1985.

Penner, Fred. "Jim Along Josie" from *Fred Penner's Place.* Oak Street Music, 1988.

Sharon, Lois, and Bram. "Jenny Jenkins" and "John Jacob Jingleheimer Schmidt" from *Smorgasbord.* Elephant Records, 1979.

Various Performers. "Jack and Jill" from *Disney's Children's Favorites, Vol. 4.* Walt Disney Records, 1990.

Various Performers. "John Jacob Jingleheimer Schmidt" from *Car Songs: Songs to Sing Anywhere.* Kimbo, 1990.

44

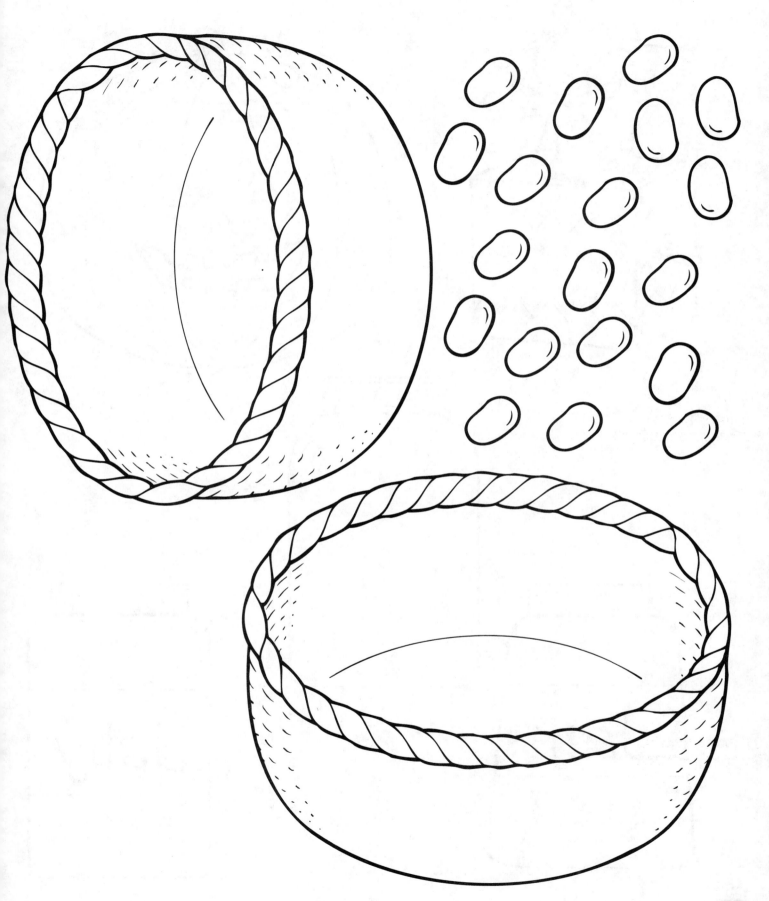

Jam

Jelly

K

Old King Cole

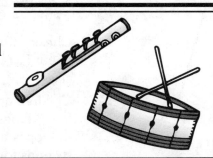

Old King Cole was a merry old soul
And a merry old soul was he.
He called for his flute,
He called for his drum,
And he called for his fiddlers three.

Talk About
What do you think a king would do all day? Old King Cole was happy and must have enjoyed his job. Invite the children to help list the jobs a king would need to do every day. Some fun ideas might be: feed the fish in the moat, take the dragon for a walk and count the jewels in the crown. If there were a King of the Class, what might his or her jobs be? Make another list of jobs a class king would need to perform to keep the classroom running smoothly. The king might need to help children line up, take messages to other "kingdoms" or choose a song to sing at group time.

Props/Visual Aids
Use the patterns on page 49 to make crowns. Choose several children to be kings each day, dividing the time evenly between them. Make sure each child gets to perform at least one of the kingly tasks during his or her reign.

To Extend This Circle Time
Create a kingdom for the kings to rule. Have the children give suggestions for the name of your kingdom. Where are the kingdom's boundaries? What are some rules that must be followed in the kingdom? Use chart paper to draw a large map of your kingdom. Show the most important features of the kingdom and how to enter and leave it.

Songs

"Kookaburra"
"Let's Go Fly a Kite"
"Three Little Kittens"

Snacks

fruit and cheese kabobs
kernels of corn
ketchup
kielbasa
any king-sized, extra large serving
kiwi fruit

Additional Activities

Make **kites** with the children by decorating pieces of construction paper that have been cut into large diamond shapes. Tape two straws in a cross to each kite and tie a 24" (61 cm) length of string or yarn to the straws. Add crepe paper streamers for a tail and invite the children outside to "fly" their kites.

Check with your local park and recreation department or YMCA for information about **karate** classes. Invite an instructor or student to give a demonstration to your class.

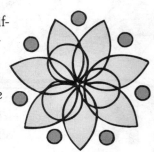

Children are fascinated by **kaleidoscopes**. There are many different types, many of them inexpensive. Bring in several kaleidoscopes and divide the children into groups. Allow about 20 seconds for each child in each group to look through the kaleidoscope and describe to the rest of the children what he or she sees as the kaleidoscope is turned. Repeat until each child has had a chance to use descriptive words. What happens if the kaleidoscope is facing a light or window? A dark corner?

Bring in a variety of **keys** and locks and allow the children to experiment with them.

Have a **Kerchief** Day. Invite each child to wear a kerchief to school. How many different ways were the kerchiefs worn? Demonstrate how a cowboy might wear a kerchief over his face to keep the dust out, how a woman with long hair might pull it back with a kerchief. In what other ways might a kerchief be useful? For what is a handkerchief used?

Books to Share

Galdone, Paul. *Three Little Kittens*. Clarion Books, 1986. Colorful illustrations help tell the familiar story of the three careless kittens, their mittens and pie.

Derby, Sally. *King Kenrick's Splinter*. Walker and Company, 1994. King Kenrick tries to ignore the painful splinter in his toe, but he finally agrees to have it attended to so that he can lead the Hero's Day parade. Rich paintings complement the humorous story.

Fox, Mem. *Koala Lou*. Harcourt Brace Jovanovich, 1988. Koala Lou longs to hear her mother speak lovingly as she did before she became so busy with brothers and sisters, so Koala Lou devises a plan to win her attention. Wonderful humorous illustrations of many Australian animals.

Gibbons, Gail. *Catch the Wind!* Little, Brown and Company, 1989. Katie and John visit Ike's Kite Shop and learn about kites and how to fly them. The informative text is accompanied by brightly colored illustrations and also includes instructions for building a kite.

Hughes, Shirley. *Alfie Gets in First*. Lothrop, Lee & Shepard Books, 1981. Alfie accidentally locks Mother and baby sister Annie Rose outside without Mother's key and can't reach the latch to let them in. Soon the whole neighborhood is involved in getting the door open.

Tapes and CDs

Glazer, Tom. "Old King Cole" from *Tom Glazer Sings Winnie the Pooh and Mother Goose*. Gateway Records/RTV Communications Group, Inc., 1991.

Jackson, Mike, and Michelle. "Kookaburra Sits," "Kookaburra Laughed" and "Emu and Kookaburra" from *Playmates*. Elephant Records, 1983.

Sharon, Lois, and Bram. "Old King Cole" and "Three Little Kittens" from *Mainly Mother Goose: Songs and Rhymes for Merry Young Souls*. Elephant Records, 1984.

Various Performers. "Kookaburra" from *Disney's Children's Favorites, Vol. 4*. Walt Disney Records, 1990.

Wellington, Bill. "Old King Cole" from *WOOF'S Greatest Bits*. Well-In-Tune Productions, 1993.

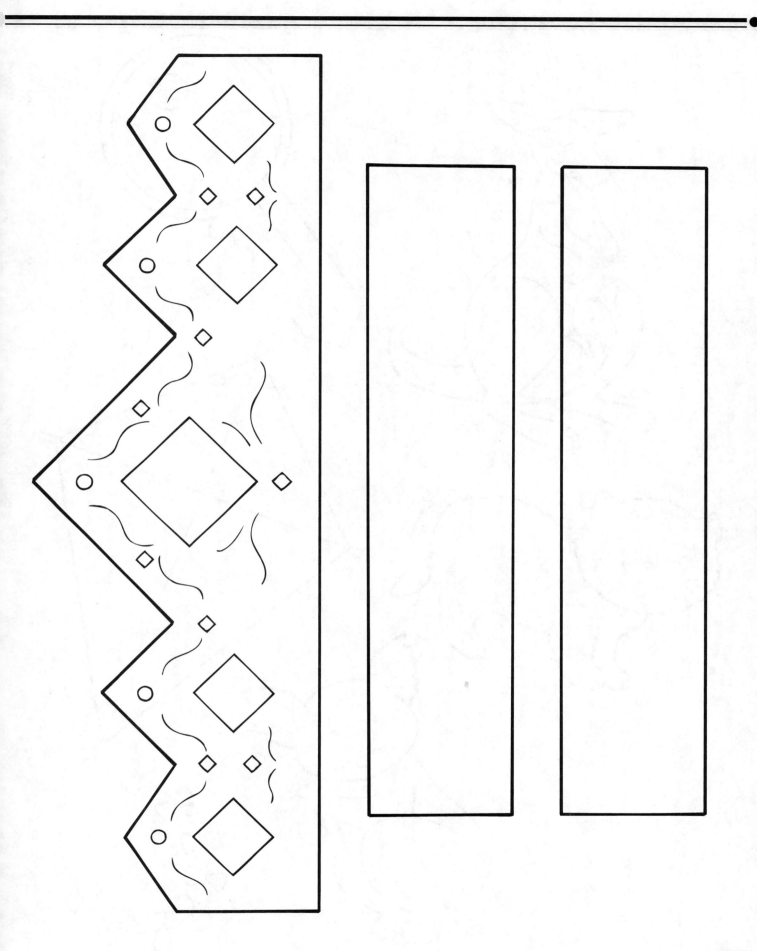

50

L

Looby Loo

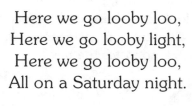

Here we go looby loo,
Here we go looby light,
Here we go looby loo,
All on a Saturday night.

Verse:

I put my left hand in,
I put my left hand out,
I give my hand a shake, shake, shake
And turn myself about.

Talk About

Invite the children to stand or sit in a circle as you sing this song. Collect a variety of things beginning with "L," using real items whenever possible. You may decide to use the clip art on page 53. Have enough items so each child will have at least one to hold. Sing the song varying the verses to name each child's "L" item. You might sing, "I put my red leaf in" or "I put the lemon out." The entire group may move in a circle as they sing the chorus.

Props/Visual Aids

Use grocery-size paper bags to make vests for the children to wear as they sing the song. Cut each bag down the back and around the bottom to make a neck opening. Cut an armhole on each side. Invite the children to decorate their bags with "L" pictures, cut from magazines or enlarge the clip art on page 53.

To Extend This Circle Time

Copy the clip art on colored paper so you will have several colors of an "L" picture. Give each child a set of the pictures. Sing the song again varying the words to create a sorting activity. You might sing, "I put the red leaf in" as each child chooses the correct color. Use a copy machine to create several sizes of the "L" pictures, and invite each child to "Put the littlest lion in" and so on.

Songs

"Did You Ever See a Lassie?"
"I Know an Old Lady"
"London Bridge"
"Skip to My Lou"
"This Land Is Your Land"

Snacks

lasagna
lemon bars or yogurt
lemonade
lentils
lettuce
licorice
lime

51

Additional Activities

Gather together a collection of "**little**" things. You might have tiny dollhouse furniture, buttons or pebbles. Invite the children to add to the collection.

Lettuce is easy to grow in a classroom. Place soil in a plastic tub, add seeds and water, and put the tub in a sunny window. Measure the lettuce to see how fast it is growing. Does it look like lettuce in the grocery store? Bring in several varieties of lettuce. What are differences in taste, color and shape? Share the lettuce for a classroom snack. Which kind tastes the best?

Set up a class **lemonade** stand. Try making real lemonade by squeezing lemons and adding water and sugar. Sell lemonade to other classes or parents.

What kind of **leaves** can you find in your neighborhood? Take a walk and gather different types. Sort the leaves by variety and identify the type of tree from which each came. Betsy Maestro's *Why Do Leaves Change Color?* HarperCollins Publishers, 1994, has realistic drawings to help you. Make leaf rubbings of the leaves you gather by placing paper on them and gently rubbing over the paper with the side of a crayon.

Practice going **left**. Help children learn to identify their left hands and feet. Try tying a scrap of lace around their left wrists or on their left shoes. How many children in your classroom use their left hand as their dominant hand? Invite children to use their left hand throughout the day for eating, coloring, cutting and so on. Supply left-handed scissors for the children to try.

Books to Share

Carle, Eric. *The Grouchy Ladybug.* HarperCollins Publishers, 1977. A grouchy ladybug challenges everyone she meets to fight, regardless of their size. Brilliantly colored, painted collages depict her adventures.

Franco, Betsy. *Fresh Fall Leaves.* Scholastic, 1994. Brightly painted collages and simple text tell how two children play in the leaves, watch them fall, run through them and throw them into the air.

Hadithi, Mwenye. *Lazy Lion.* Little, Brown and Company, 1990. Lion is too lazy to build a home for himself before the Big Rains come, so he orders the other animals to build one for him. Bright watercolor paintings illustrate the animals who do their best to please him.

Hale, Sarah Josepha. *Mary Had a Little Lamb.* Orchard Books, 1995. Beautiful fabric relief illustrations help tell this familiar nursery rhyme. Also included is information about the history of the rhyme.

Kraus, Robert. *Leo the Late Bloomer.* Windmill Books, 1971. Leo, a young tiger, finally blooms under the anxious eyes of his father. Illustrated with whimsical ink and color drawings.

Lewis, Kim. *Emma's Lamb.* Four Winds Press, 1991. Emma looks after a little lost lamb, feeds and plays games with him and helps him find his mother. Detailed realistic illustrations.

Tapes and CDs

Greg and Steve. "Did You Ever See a Lassie?" from *Playing Favorites.* Youngheart Records, 1991.

McGrath, Bob. "London Bridge" from *Sing Along with Bob, Vol. 2.* Kids' Records, 1985.

McGrath, Bob. "Looby Loo" from *Sing Along with Bob, Vol. 1.* Kids' Records, 1984.

Penner, Fred. "Skip to My Lou" and "This Land Is Your Land" from *A House for Me.* Troubadour Records Ltd./Oak Street Music, 1985, 1991.

Sharon, Lois, and Bram. "Looby Loo" from *One Elephant, Deux Elephants.* Elephant Records, 1980.

M

Braille

Miss Mary Mack

Miss Mary Mack, Mack, Mack
All dressed in black, black, black
With silver buttons, buttons, buttons
All down her back, back, back
She asked her mother, mother, mother
For fifteen cents, cents, cents
To see the elephants, elephants, elephants
Jump over the fence, fence, fence
They jumped so high, high, high
They touched the sky, sky, sky
And didn't come back, back, back
'Til the Fourth of July, July, July.

Talk About

In this song we sing about *Miss* Mary Mack. Share other titles that come before people's names. Mary might have chosen to be called *Ms.* Mary Mack. If she was married, she might wish to be called *Mrs.* Mary Mack. Marty Mack might be *Mr.*, and several generations ago young boys were formally addressed as *Master.* Invite the children to choose the title they would like to be called for the rest of the day.

Props/Visual Aids

Use the patterns on page 56 to make name cards to help the children remember which title they have chosen.

To Extend This Circle Time

Using a title to address a person often indicates good manners or respect. What are some other manners or respectful behaviors? Invite the children to help you make a list of manners. What manners do their parents expect at home? Try to practice the manners, especially at snack time. Then make a list of silly manners.
For example: When you take a giraffe to the movies, always sit in the back row.

"Do You Know the Muffin Man?"
"I See the Moon"
"Mary Had a Little Lamb"
"Mulberry Bush"
"Old MacDonald Had a Farm"
"Three Blind Mice"

M & M's® in cookies or as decoration
macaroni
marshmallows
meat loaf
mozzarella cheese
muffins
mushrooms
mustard

54

Additional Activities

Make simple **masks** with the children. Use paper plates, yarn, construction paper scraps, large craft sticks, tape and glue. Precut eye holes in the plates and invite the children to decorate them with yarn and paper to make funny or scary masks. Tape the craft stick securely to the plate for a handle.

Place a variety of **magnets** and objects (some metal) on your science table. Which objects attract the magnets? Help the children record their findings on the chart on page 57.

If your children have access to a computer, use this opportunity to reinforce skill in using the **mouse**.

M & M's® are a perfect treat for the letter "M" and can be used to teach a number of skills. After washing hands and the table, give each child 15 M & M's®. Count them, sort them by color and create simple patterns or shapes. Can the children form an "M"? Then invite the children to **munch**!

Children are very interested in the **moon**. Often, it is visible during the day. Share a story, such as Laura Jane Coats' *Marcella and the Moon*, Macmillan Publishing Company, 1986, that shows the moon's phases. Record on your class calendar when the moon is full. What is it like on the moon? Talk about the missions to the moon and some of the things that were learned.

Books to Share

Allen, Jonathan. *Mucky Moose*. Macmillan Publishing Company, 1990. Mucky is the smelliest, yuck moose in the forest which comes in handy when the fiercest wolf in the forest decides to eat Mucky for dinner.

Babcock, Chris. *No Moon, No Milk!* Crown, 1993. Martha the cow refuses to give milk unless she can visit the moon like her great-great-grandmother, the cow who jumped over the moon.

Gackenbach, Dick. *Mag the Magnificent*. Clarion Books, 1985. A boy's drawing on the wall of a magical monster sets off a series of adventures for the two of them, until his mother wants the wall cleaned off.

Ivimey, John W. *The Complete Story of the Three Blind Mice*. Clarion Books, 1987. This version of the familiar song includes many new stanzas and a happy ending.

Kraus, Robert. *Musical Max*. Simon & Schuster, Inc., 1990. When Musical Max loses the mood for making music, the peace and quiet drives the neighbors just as crazy as his constant practicing did.

Porter, Susan. *Moose Music*. Western Publishing Company, Inc., 1994. No one appreciates the noisy music moose makes when he plays his fiddle until a lady moose hears him and sings along. Bright and humorous illustrations.

Rogers, Jean. *Runaway Mittens*. Greenwillow Books, 1988. Pica's mittens are always turning up in strange places, but when he finds them keeping the newborn puppies warm in their box, he decides that they are in exactly the right place.

Tapes and CDs

Beall, Pamela, and Susan Hagen Nipp. "Old MacDonald Had a Farm" from *Wee Sing Children's Songs and Fingerplays*. Price Stern Sloan, 1990.

Jenkins, Ella. "May-Ree-Mack" and "Miss Mary Mack" from *You'll Sing a Song and I'll Sing a Song*. Smithsonian/Folkways, 1989.

Koch, Fred. "May-Ree-Mack," "Miss Mary Mack" and "Miss Mary Mack (Pennsylvania version)" from *Did You Feed My Cow?* Red Rover Records, 1989.

Sharon, Lois, and Bram. "Mary Had a Little Lamb" and "Three Blind Mice" from *Mainly Mother Goose: Songs and Rhymes for Merry Young Souls*. Elephant Records, 1984.

Master

_____

_____

_____

Mr.

_____

_____

Miss

_____

_____

_____

Ms.

_____

_____

My Magnet . . .

no

I Love Noodles

To the tune of "The Eensy Weensy Spider"
Noodles in the morning
Noodles in the night
Noodles on my plate
I eat up every bite
Shells or macaroni
I sprinkle them with cheese
So when I sit down at mealtime
It's "Pass the noodles, please!"

Talk About

There are many shapes and varieties of noodles. Cook up a big pot of different types and have a taste test with your class. Which shapes are most popular? Which flavor is the favorite? Make a simple graph to show the children's responses. If time allows, talk about and graph the children's favorite toppings for noodles: red sauce, white sauce, gravy, cheese or butter.

Props/Visual Aids

Reproduce, color and laminate the noodle cards on page 61 to make pairs of matching cards. Mix the cards and invite the children to play a matching game. Then supply real noodles and have the children match the real noodles to their picture cards.

We Love Noodles!			
Drew			
Carlos			
Kirby		Adam	
Allix		Min	
Lauren	Cahlor	Leesha	Tommy

To Extend This Circle Time

Bring in a pasta-making machine to make fresh noodles with the children. Invite parents to join you for a nourishing noodle lunch. Dried noodles can be used for a variety of art projects. You may wish to color the noodles first, by dipping them in a small dish of food coloring diluted with water. Allow the noodles to dry on waxed paper and provide string for noodle necklaces or glue and paper for noodle collages.

Songs
"I'm a Nut"
"No More Pie"
"The North Wind Doth Blow"
"Now the Day Is Over, Night Is Drawing Nigh"

Snacks
nachos
nectarines
noodles
nuts (Be aware of any allergies to nuts and that nuts may pose a choking hazard.)

Additional Activities

Start a collection of **nickels** in a see-through plastic jar. Invite the children to estimate how many nickels have been added to the jar and after a specified time, count the nickels and use them to buy a special item for the classroom.

Create a class **newspaper**. Invite the children to dictate stories and draw pictures to tell what is happening in their room, the playground or other class events. Write the articles on newsprint and post the pages in the hallway for parents to read.

Talk about **noise**! Share one of many stories about noisy children (see Books to Share below). When does your class make the most noise? When are the children very quiet? Supply each child with a party noisemaker. Practice making noise at the same time and then stopping at your signal. What are some other ways to make noise?

What's in a **name**? Bring in a name book and help the children find their names. Write the names and their meanings on chart paper. Are there any names that are not found in the book? Invite the children's parents to share the special meanings of any unusual names they may have.

Books to Share

Caple, Kathy. *The Biggest Nose.* Houghton Mifflin Company, 1985. Eleanor the elephant is sensitive about being teased because she has the biggest nose in school.

Compton, Kenn, and Joanne. *Granny Greenteeth & the Noise in the Night.* Holiday House, 1993. When no one will help Granny find out what's making the noise under her bed, she starts a chain reaction that brings results. Humorous illustrations depict the quirky characters.

Machotka, Hana. *Breathtaking Noses.* Morrow Junior Books, 1992. Fascinating facts and clear colorful photographs examine the noses of a variety of animals and describe how they function.

Rann, Toni. *My First Look at Numbers.* Random House, 1990. Bright photographs of objects introduce the concept of numbers and counting, from one teddy bear to 100 candies.

Wells, Rosemary. *Noisy Nora.* Dial Press, 1973. Feeling neglected, Nora makes more and more noise to attract her parents' attention.

Winthrop, Elizabeth. *A Very Noisy Girl.* Holiday House, 1991. Elizabeth is a very noisy girl, but her mother begins to miss her exuberance when she pretends to be a very quiet dog.

Tapes and CDs

Barolk Folk with Madeline MacNeil, and Barbara Hess. "The North Wind Doth Blow" from *Girls and Boys, Come out to Play.* Music for Little People, 1991.

Beall, Pamela Conn, and Susan Hagen Nipp. "I'm a Nut" from *Wee Sing Silly Songs.* Price Stern Sloan, 1986.

Beall, Pamela Conn, and Susan Hagen Nipp. "Now the Day Is Over" from *Wee Sing Sing-Alongs.* Price Stern Sloan, 1982.

Jenkins, Ella. "No More Pie" from *Adventures in Rhythm.* Smithsonian/Folkways Records, 1989.

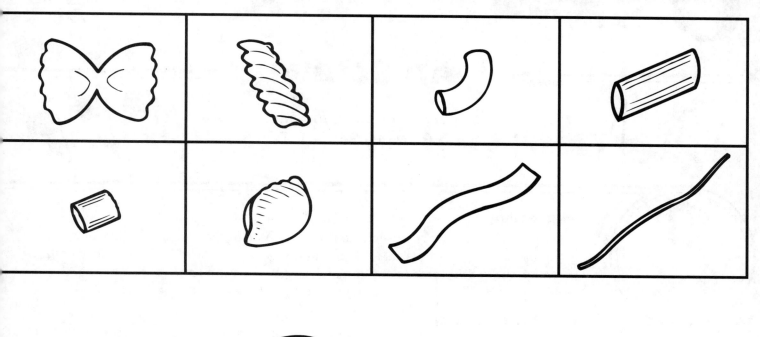

O

International Morse Code

Braille

An Octave

Sing the song up or down the musical scale.
Do Re Mi Fa So La Ti Do

Talk About

The words in this song represent the notes in an octave, a series of eight notes going up or down the musical scale. Sing the octave to warm up your voices in the morning. Vary the words to the song by singing the numbers 1 to 8, letters of the alphabet: A-B-C-D-E-F-G-A, the names of the children or just the letter "O."

Props/Visual Aids

Teach your class the hand signs for the notes in the octave. Reproduce the illustrations on page 64 to use as visual reminders as you sing.

To Extend This Circle Time

Create hand signs for another simple children's song. You might sing:

Row, row, row your boat	*Make rowing motions with both arms*
Gently down the stream	*Move hand up and down for gently flowing water*
Merrily, merrily, merrily, merrily,	*Laugh silently*
Life is but a dream.	*Pretend to sleep, head to side resting on hands*

Invite the children to create signs for a chosen song. Record their ideas on chart paper to sing again and again.

Songs

"Oats, Peas, Beans and Barley Grow"
"One Light, One Sun"
"Open Them, Shut Them"
"Oranges and Lemons"
"Over in the Meadow"
"Over the River and Through the Woods"

Snacks

oatmeal cookies
olives
omelets
onion-flavored
    crackers or dip
oranges
O-shaped oat cereal

Additional Activities

Bring in a recording of **oboe** music. Check with your local high school or community band to find an oboe player who could visit your class and demonstrate how to play his or her instrument. Be sure to ask for an octave!

An **opera** is a story told with music. Introduce and then listen to an opera while the children are having snack or free time.

Set up an **office** in your dramatic play area. Supply pads of paper, account ledgers, calculators, pens and pencils, and an old typewriter. Parents who work in an office environment may be able to supply additional props.

Take a field trip to an **orchard**.

Explore the concepts of **off** and **on**. Bring in a variety of switches and knobs and collect any toys or props that can be turned "off" and "on." Assign the responsibility of turning the classroom lights off and on to a different child each day. What would happen if you left the water on in the bathroom? What if you turned the furnace off in the winter? Play a variation of the game Red Light, Green Light with your class. Use a flashlight to signal "on," and invite the children to move about the room. When you turn the flashlight off, the children must freeze in place.

Books to Share

Burton, Marilee Robin. *Oliver's Birthday.* Harper & Row Publishers, 1986. Oliver the ostrich is convinced his friends have forgotten his birthday when no one seems to come to help him celebrate.

Brandenberg, Franz. *Otto Is Different.* Greenwillow Books, 1985. Otto the Octopus learns to appreciate the advantages of having eight arms instead of only two.

Edwards, Richard. *Ten Tall Oaktrees.* Tambourine Books, 1993. Vibrant pictures and rhythmic verse describe how one by one a grove of oak trees disappears in the endless cycle of change that nature and humankind create.

Kunhardt, Edith. *I'm Going to Be a Police Officer.* Scholastic, Inc., 1995. Bright photographs and clear text explain Michelle's dad's busy day as a police officer.

Marshak, Suzanna. *I Am the Ocean.* Arcade Publishing, 1991. In this lyrical narrative, the ocean sings of itself, its many creatures, its strength and beauty. Colorful, detailed illustrations show the ocean's inhabitants, great and small, from whales to animals so small they live in a drop of water.

Tapes and CDs

Barolk Folk with Madeline MacNeil, and Barbara Hess. "Oranges and Lemons" from *Girls and Boys, Come out to Play.* Music for Little People, 1991.

Merrill Staton Children's Voices. "Oats, Peas, Beans" from *Music 1 . . . 2 . . . 3, Vol. 3: Singing Games and Dances.* Columbia Special Products, 1977.

Monet, Lisa. "Open/Shut Them" from *Circle Time: Songs and Rhymes for the Very Young.* Monet Productions, 1986.

Raffi. "Oats and Beans and Barley" and "Over in the Meadow" from *Baby Beluga.* Troubadour Records, 1977.

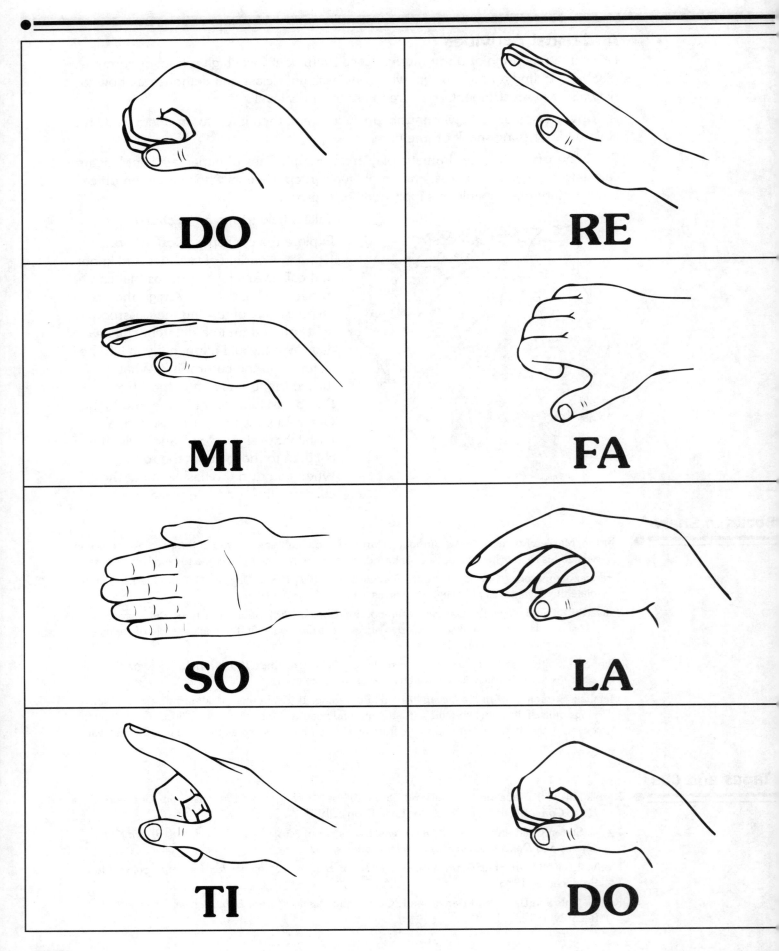

DO

RE

MI

FA

SO

LA

TI

DO

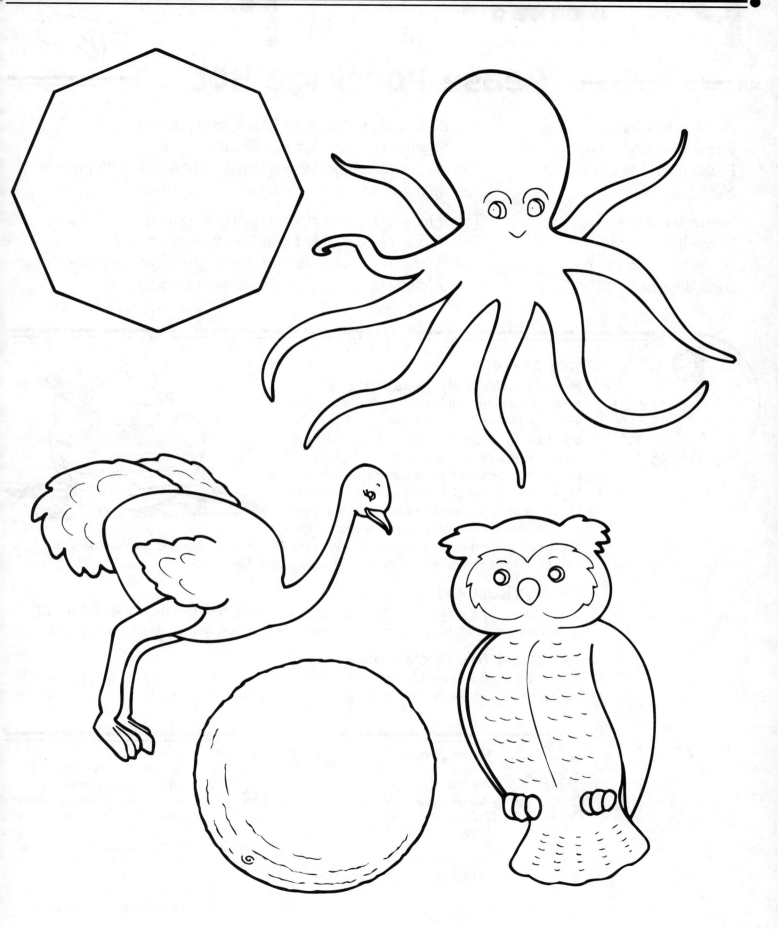

P

International Morse Code

Braille

Pease Porridge Hot

Pease porridge hot	*Tap thighs, clap, slap right hands with partner*
Pease porridge cold	*Tap thighs, clap, slap left hands with partner*
Pease porridge in the pot	*Tap thighs, clap, slap left and then right hands with partner*
Nine days old	*Tap thighs, clap, slap right hands with partner*
Some like it hot	*Tap thighs, clap, slap right hands with partner*
Some like it cold	*Tap thighs, clap, slap left hands with partner*
Some like it in the pot	*Tap thighs, clap, slap left and then right hands with partner*
Nine days old	*Tap thighs, clap, slap right hands with partner*

Talk About

Have the children sit in pairs, facing each other. Invite the children to tap their thighs and clap their hands together and with each other as you sing the song. Ask the children if they have ever eaten porridge. Explain that oatmeal could be considered porridge. How many of the children like oatmeal hot? Cold? Would anyone like oatmeal nine days old? A well-known story has "too cold," "too hot" and "just right" porridge in it. Invite the children to help you tell "Goldilocks and the Three Bears" by placing the pieces on the flannel board.

Props/Visual Aids

Reproduce, color and cut out the illustrations on page 68. Use double-sided tape to attach scraps of felt to the back of the pieces so they will adhere to a flannel board.

To Extend This Circle Time

Instant oatmeal is available commercially in many flavors and is easy to prepare in the classroom. Make several varieties and have a "porridge" snack.

Songs

"Higglety, Pigglety, Pop"
"I Know a Little Pussy"
"Paw Paw Patch"
"Peanut Butter and Jelly"
"Puff, the Magic Dragon"
"Pussycat, Pussycat"

Snacks

pancakes
pasta (different shapes) sprinkled
   with parmesan cheese
peaches, pears, pineapple, plums
peanut butter in pita pocket bread
   or popovers
peas, pickles, potatoes
pie made with pudding
pizza
popcorn, pretzels
pumpkin—cookies, bars or pie

Additional Activities

Many of the "P" snacks are foods the children can help you prepare in class. You might use frozen bread dough to make **pretzels**. Follow the directions on the package for thawing, and allow the children to shape pieces of dough on waxed paper. Transfer the pretzels to cookie sheets, bake as directed and enjoy!

Have a class **parade**. Help the children roll a sheet of newspaper tightly and tape it to make a narrow, sturdy "tube." Tape or staple crepe paper streamers to one end of the newspaper roll. The children will enjoy holding their "banners" high as they march.

Make **paint**! Try one of these non-cook recipes with your children:

- Pour liquid starch on a piece of paper. Sprinkle on powdered tempera paint and mix.
- Pour one cup (240 ml) water in a bowl. Add wheat paste slowly, stirring constantly until it is the consistency of whipped cream. Mix in powdered tempera paint.
- Mix soap powder with a little water to make a smooth paste. Add powdered tempera paint and whip until stiff, if desired.

Place **pom-poms** in your sensory table. Supply cups to sort the pom-poms by size or color. Glue pom-poms on purple or pink paper cut into "P"s.

Plan a **Pajama** Day. Invite the children to wear their pajamas and bring their pillows to school.

Books to Share

Calmenson, Stephanie. *Dinner at the Panda Palace*. HarperCollins Publishers, 1991. Mr. Panda, owner of the Panda Palace restaurant, manages to find seating for all of his animal patrons on a very busy night.

Enderle, Judith Ross. *A Pile of Pigs*. Boyds Mills Press, 1993. Following his curiosity, littlest pig has all the pigs climb pig by pig by pig to form a pyramid to look over the other side of the barn.

McMillan, Bruce. *Puffins Climb, Penguins Rhyme*. Harcourt Brace & Company, 1995. Beautiful color photographs illustrate simple rhyming verses and introduce readers to puffins and penguins in the wild.

Omerand, Jan. *Midnight Pillow Fight*. Candlewick Press, 1993. When Polly's pillow wants to play in the middle of the night, they have a romp and things get a little out of hand.

Rylant, Cynthia. *Mr. Putter and Tabby Pick the Pears*. Harcourt Brace & Company, 1995. Mr. Putter is too old to climb the ladder to pick his pears, but he and his cat find an ingenious way to pick pears for pear jelly. Humorous, colorful watercolor illustrations.

Titherington, Jeanne. *Pumpkin, Pumpkin*. Greenwillow Books, 1986. Jamie plants a pumpkin seed and watches it grow from a sprout to a plant. When he carves his pumpkin, he saves six seeds to plant in the spring. Beautiful, realistic drawings help tell the story.

Zolotow, Charlotte. *Peter and the Pigeons*. Greenwillow Books, 1993. After seeing all the animals in the zoo, Peter still likes the pigeons he sees every day the best. Soft, colored pencil illustrations.

Tapes and CDs

Peter, Paul, and Mary. "Puff, the Magic Dragon" from *Peter, Paul and Mommy, Too*. Warner Brothers, 1993.

Scruggs, Joe. "Peas Porridge Hot" from *Bahamas Pajamas*. Shadow Play Records, 1990.

Sharon, Lois, and Bram. "I Know a Little Pussy" from *Singing 'n' Swinging*. Elephant Records, 1980.

Sharon, Lois, and Bram. "Paw Paw Patch" from *One Elephant, Deux Elephants*. Elephant Records, 1980.

Sharon, Lois, and Bram. "Peanut Butter and Jelly" from *Great Big Hits*. A & M Records, 1992.

Q

Braille

The Quiet Song

To the tune of "Twinkle, Twinkle, Little Star"
I am being very quiet
Quiet as a little mouse
You won't hear me make a sound
Am I even in the house?
I am being very quiet
Quiet as a little mouse.

Talk About

Sing the song very quietly. Talk with your class about being quiet and quiet times. How do you know if someone wants you to be quiet? What are some words or signals that mean "please be quiet"? Play a quiet game with your children. You may wish to put on some quiet music for a calming effect, and then invite everyone to lie down on the floor. Tell the children that you will walk carefully all around them to see who is being the quietest. Gently tap that child on the shoulder, and he or she may select the next quietest person. Join the game by taking the child's place on the floor. Play until everyone has had a turn or you sense that the children are ready for a new activity. Be sure to tell the children that the game will be ending soon; "Three more quiet kids and the game will be over."

Props/Visual Aids

Use the illustrations on page 73 to make quiet signs for your classroom. Invite the children to help you decide where or when the signs should be displayed. Reproduce a small sign for each child so they may let others know when they wish to work quietly.

To Extend This Circle Time

Give each child a rhythm instrument such as jingle bells, sand blocks, sticks, finger cymbals, drum, maracas, tambourine and so on. Make your own simple instruments if necessary. Shakers are easily made by putting beans, rice or pebbles in empty film canisters with tight-fitting lids. Tambourines can be constructed by placing a handful of beans inside small paper plates and stapling or taping the plates together. Your wooden building blocks can also make a great percussion sound. After the children have explored their instruments, practice playing the instruments very quietly. Then play the instruments loudly. Which do they think sound better? Sing the song again with quiet instrument accompaniment.

Songs

"Quack, Quack"
"The Queen of Hearts"
"Questions"
"Quiet"

Snacks

fruit cut into quarters
quesadillas
quiche
quick bread

Additional Activities

Make a classroom **quilt**. Depending on the age and skill level of your children, you can make a very simple pattern or one that is more complicated. For a simple paper "quilt," give each child a square of paper. Help the children choose a theme for the quilt and supply markers, paint or crayons for them to decorate their squares. When the squares are completed, lay out the pattern of the quilt on the floor. Have the children help in deciding where their squares should be placed. Tape the squares together securely on the back and display the finished quilt on a wall. For a more complicated activity, give each child a square of plain fabric. Provide fabric markers or have the child take his or her square home for families to decorate together. Again, when the squares are completed, lay out the quilt's design as a class. If possible, arrange for a parent to sew the squares together and add a backing.

The prefixes **quar** or **quad** can mean "four" as in **quadruplets**, **quarter** or **quartet**. Divide the children into groups of four for some of your routine activities. Reproduce the pattern on page 72. Accordion-fold a large piece of butcher paper three times to make four areas of paper the same width as the pattern. Trace the pattern and cut it out to make four connected large paper dolls. Invite each quartet of children to color a set of quadruplets. Display them in your Letter of the Week area.

Collect quotable **quotes** from the children in your classroom. Record them in a book to share with parents.

Children love to ask **questions**. Each day, write a Question of the Day on a large sheet of chart paper. Throughout the day, invite children to write or dictate possible answers to the question. At the end of the day, share the answers with the children. You will want to make some of your questions open-ended with many "correct" answers and other questions just for fun, such as "Why is an orange orange?" or "How did the elephant get such a long nose?"

Make **quarter** collages. Supply the children with different sized squares, rectangles and circles of colored construction paper, each divided by dotted lines into four equal pieces. Help the children cut the pieces on the lines to make the quarters and glue all four pieces of each shape on another piece of paper in any design.

Books to Share

Cole, Barbara Hancock. *Texas Star*. Orchard Books, 1990. There's a lot to do to get ready for the quilters to come, and Papa grumbles that the family doesn't need another quilt. The quilters finish it just in time for the first snow of the winter, and then Papa is happy that he helped.

Merriam, Eve. *Quiet, Please*. Simon & Schuster, 1993. Simple, poetic text and beautiful paintings present reflections on quiet moments in nature, from mushrooms sprouting in the gentle rain to moonlight making a checkerboard on a brick wall.

Offen, Hilda. *As Quiet as a Mouse*. Dutton's Children's Books, 1994. This action rhyme begins with "I was as quiet as a mouse" but builds to a tumult beginning with a butterfly's sigh and ending with a dinosaur roar. Finally, a song calms the uproar once again and everyone quietly dances.

Parnell, Peter. *Quiet*. Morrow Junior Books, 1989. A child lies so quietly on the ground that Raven, Chipmunk and finally Chickadee come to his side.

Rogers, Paul, and Emma. *Quacky Duck*. Little, Brown and Company, 1995. This rhyming story is about a duck who was very fond of quacking at everything and everyone, but when she stops quacking, things just aren't the same.

Tapes and CDs

Carfa, Pat. "Quack, Quack" from *Songs for Sleepy Heads and Out-of-Beds!* Lullaby Lady Productions, 1984.

Roth, Kevin. "Quiet Times" from *Lullabies for Little Dreamers*. CMS Records, Inc., 1985.

Sesame Street Muppets. "The Question Song" from *The Muppet Alphabet Album*. Sesame Street Records/Golden, 1971.

Smith, Janet. "The Lost Quarter" and "Quiet" from *I'm a Delightful Child*. Pacific Cascade Records, 1977.

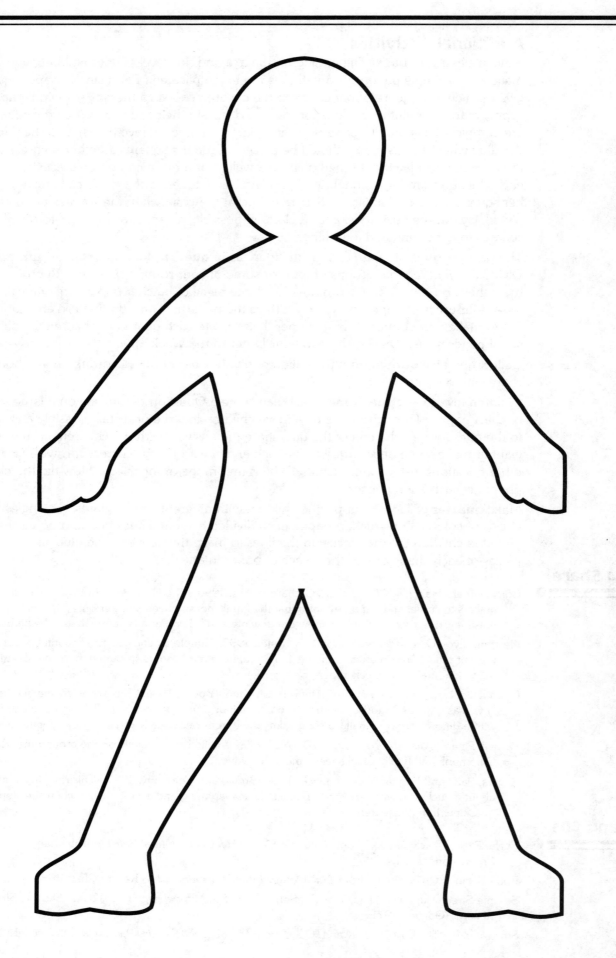

 shhh! # QUIET, PLEASE!

QUIET!

R

International Morse Code

Braille

Row, Row, Row Your Boat

Row, row, row your boat
Gently down the stream
Merrily, merrily, merrily, merrily,
Life is but a dream.

Talk About

This can be a very relaxing song. Invite the children to lie on the floor and pretend they are floating in a boat down the stream. Have them gently rock back and forth as the waves move the boat. Can they hear the water burbling over the rocks? Is the sun shining brightly? Where will the stream take them? Write the children's ideas about their adventures and provide paper for illustrations. Bind the stories together in a book.

Props/Visual Aids

Again, emphasize the gentleness of the song's flowing. Divide the children into partners, and give each pair a towel. Invite the children to sit facing their partners, each grasping one end of the towel. Sing the song again as the children gently pull, leaning forward and back, alternating with their partners and using the towel between them as support.

To Extend This Circle Time

Invite the children to bring in their toy boats for a regatta in your water table. Which boats would need rowing to win the race?

Songs
"I Can Sing a Rainbow"
"It's Raining; It's Pouring"
"I've Been Working on the Railroad"
"Rain, Rain, Go Away"
"Ring Around the Rosey"

Snacks
radishes
raisins
raspberries or raspberry
   jam on round crackers
ravioli
rhubarb
rice
rice cakes
rolls (raisin or rye)
root beer

74

Additional Activities

Make a class **recipe** book. Have the children dictate their recollections of favorite recipes. Invite them to illustrate the finished recipes and share the book with parents.

Raffia is an interesting craft material to add to your supply closet. Bring it out occasionally for the children to use in their art projects.

Listen to the **radio** during free choice time. Check out the stations in your area; there may be a station that specializes in children's programming for all or part of the day. Arrange a field trip to visit a radio station.

Set up a round **relay race** for the children to run. Give each team a red ribbon to hand off, and have groups of children stationed around the perimeter of a large open area. The "race" will be much like running the bases in baseball. Emphasize cooperation rather than competition as much as possible.

Discuss **recycling** with your children. What are the items that can be recycled in your area? What happens to the paper, bottles, cardboard, plastic, etc., when they are recycled? Where would they go if they were not recycled? Set up, label and use recycling containers in your classroom.

Books to Share

Baker, Susan. *First Look at Rivers*. Gareth Stevens Children's Books, 1991. Clear, colorful photographs and simple text explain how rivers begin, travel and end, and how they benefit humankind.

Carlson, Nancy. *Loudmouth George and the Big Race*. Carolrhoda Books, 1983. George the rabbit brags, procrastinates and offers excuses instead of training for the big race.

Dooley, Nora. *Everybody Cooks Rice*. Carolrhoda Books, 1991. Everyone in this multiethnic neighborhood is fixing rice for dinner–each family in their own special and unique way.

Gilliland, Judith Heide. *River*. Clarion Books, 1993. Watercolor illustrations and poetic text describe the mightiest river in the world, the Amazon and the life it supports in its rain forests.

Otto, Carolyn. *That Sky, That Rain*. Thomas Y. Crowell, 1990. As a rainstorm approaches, a young girl and her grandfather take the farm animals into the shelter of the barn and then watch the rain begin.

Serfozo, Mary. *Rain Talk*. Margaret K. McElderry Books, 1990. Beautiful watercolor paintings and descriptive text show the pleasures of a rainy day for a little girl and her dog.

Smith, Cara Lockhart. *Twenty-Six Rabbits Run Riot*. Little, Brown and Company, 1990. Mrs. Fitzwarren has 26 very naughty children and a day's outing with this rambunctious bunch soon turns chaotic when Baby keeps hiding. Very detailed illustrations depict the rabbits' antics, from dancing on the mantle to climbing the curtains, and readers can join in the search for Baby.

Wellington, Monica. *Night Rabbits*. Dutton's Children's Books, 1995. This simple story with brightly colored illustrations tells of two little rabbits on a nighttime adventure, nibbling in the garden, running from the red fox, listening to raindrops and finally scurrying home to sleep.

Tapes and CDs

Greg and Steve. "Ain't Gonna Rain No More" and "Rain, Rain, Go Away" from *Playing Favorites*. Youngheart Records, 1991.

Jenkins, Ella. "It's Raining Cats and Dogs" and "Rain, Rain, Go Away" from *My Street Begins at My House and Other Songs and Rhythms from "The Me Too Show."* Smithsonian/Folkways Records, 1989.

Penner, Fred. "Red, Red Robin" from *Happy Feet*. Oak Street Music, 1991.

Roth, Kevin. "It Ain't Gonna Rain No More"; "I've Been Working on the Railroad" and "Row, Row, Row Your Boat" from *Oscar, Bingo and Buddies*. CMS Records, Inc., 1986.

Various Performers. "It Ain't Gonna Rain No More"; "I've Been Working on the Railroad" and "Row, Row, Row Your Boat" from *Disney's Children's Favorites, Vol. 1*. Walt Disney Productions, 1979.

Various Performers. "Ring Around the Rosey" from *Disney's Children's Favorites, Vol. 3*. Walt Disney Records, 1986.

75

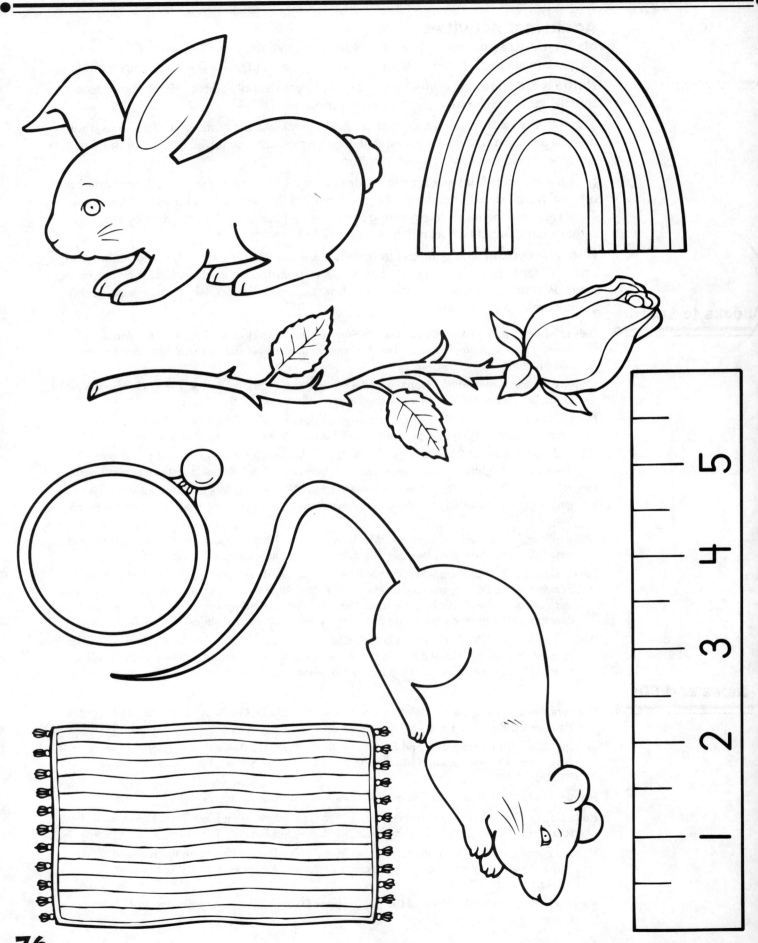

76

S

Braille

Sing a Song of Sixpence

Sing a song of sixpence, a pocketful of rye
Four and twenty blackbirds baked in a pie
When the pie was opened the birds began to sing
Wasn't that a sight to see and set before the king?

S

Talk About

The king must have been very surprised to find 24 singing birds in his pie! Explain that a surprise is something that happens when you don't expect it. Tell the children about a time you were surprised. Invite them to share times they were surprised.

Props/Visual Aids

Make copies of the pie patterns on page 80. Ask the children what they think a good surprise inside a pie would be. Supply washable markers or crayons and invite the children to draw their ideas on the "inside" pie piece pattern. Have them color the top pie piece and cut out both. Fasten the top and inside pie pieces together with a brad. When the pie is "opened," you will see the surprise inside!

To Extend This Circle Time

Involve your children in planning a surprise party. This will be a good time to talk about another "S" word: *secret!* Any event could be the focus of the party: a staff member's birthday, a student teacher's last day, a special time for parents. The highlight of the party will be deciding how to do the surprise. Have everyone hide under a table, in the restroom or behind a shelf. When the guest of honor arrives, jump out and yell, "Surprise!" The children will enjoy this so much, you may have to do it again and again. Use the invitation pattern on page 80 to invite more friends, staff or parents to your party.

Songs

"Itsy Bitsy Spider"
"Mr. Sun"
"A Ram Sam Sam"
"Shortnin' Bread"
"Sing When the Spirit Says Sing"
"Skinnamarink"
"Skip to My Lou"

Snacks

salad
salsa
saltines
sandwiches
soup or stew
sourdough or sesame
   seed bread
spaghetti
strawberries
sunflower seeds
sweet potatoes

Additional Activities

Have a special **Stocking** Day. Have the children wear their favorite **socks** to school. Take off your **shoes** for circle time and share what makes your socks special. Make Sock Snowpeople with old, clean white tube socks. Have each child stuff his or her sock with old nylon stockings, shredded foam or a fiberfil-type stuffing. Use a rubber band to securely fasten the opening about halfway up the ribbed ankle part of the sock. Fold the top of the sock down for the snowperson's hat and glue some scraps of yarn inside for the hat's tassel. Tie a yarn scarf around the snowperson's neck and glue on felt scraps or use markers to make the face and buttons.

Supply several grades of **sandpaper** with blocks of wood. Which sandpaper feels the most rough? Show the children how to use the sandpaper to make the wood smooth.

Give each child a **scarf** to use while moving to different types of music. You can find a variety of scarves at thrift stores, or make your own from squares of sheer fabric. Invite the children to wave their scarves using full arm movements, either back and forth or in large circles, to the rhythm of the music.

Set up a **store** in your dramatic play area. Decide with the children what kind of store you will have and what items will be for sale. You might choose to have a toy, book, food or clothing store. Have the children help in gathering props and setting up the store. Decide who will work in the store and who will be customers. Make sure everyone has had a chance to play all the roles.

Playing in **sand** is a wonderful sensory experience for children and adults. Provide scoops, shovels, buckets and molds. Allow the children to take off their shoes and socks to really experience the sand between their toes. If playing in the sand outside is not an option, bring sand in. Use a large plastic tub or your sensory table and keep the sand slightly moist to stick together. Hide items that begin with "S" in the sand for the children to find. Keep a whisk broom and dustpan handy and help the children with another "S" word: **sweeping**!

Books to Share

Buck, Nola. *Sid and Sam*. HarperCollins Publishers, 1996. This silly story is full of "S"s. Sid and Sam sing a song, but Sid's song is so long! This "I Can Read Book" has whimsical illustrations.

Conrad, Pam. *Molly and the Strawberry Day*. HarperCollins Publishers, 1994. After Molly and her parents pick strawberries, she spends the rest of the day finding new ways to enjoy them, from making jam to floating strawberries in her bath.

Dewey, Ariane. *The Sky*. Green Tiger Press, 1993. An imaginative look at the sky, both fanciful and realistic, where the sun shines or snowflakes fall, the space shuttle soars or Santa Claus flies.

Edwards, Pamela Duncan. *Some Smug Slug*. HarperCollins Publishers, 1996. This alliterative tale has a smirking and self-important slug slithering his way up a highly suspect slope, as a sparrow, spider, swallowtail, skunk, squirrel and stink bug try to stop him. Also, hidden in each of the beautiful detailed paintings is an "S" shape.

Pearson, Tracey Campbell. *The Storekeeper*. Dial Books for Young Readers, 1988. Bright illustrations and simple text follow the activities of a small town storekeeper from early morning when she opens her shop until late at night when she finally goes home.

Peterson, Jeanne Whitehouse. *My Mama Sings*. HarperCollins Publishers, 1994. Mama has special old songs for all occasions, until a day when she has no song ready and her little boy sings his own special song just for her. Beautiful, richly colored illustrations.

Ray, Deborah Kogan. *Stargazing Sky*. Crown Publishers, Inc., 1991. Luminous watercolor illustrations help tell the story of a little girl and her mother who stay up late to watch a shower of shooting stars.

Shannon, George. *The Surprise*. Greenwillow Books, 1983. Squirrel gives his mother a very special surprise on her birthday. Simple, bright watercolor and ink illustrations.

Wood, Audrey. *Silly Sally*. Harcourt Brace Jovanovich, 1992. A rhyming story of Silly Sally who makes many silly friends as she travels to town backwards and upside down.

Tapes and CDs

Barolk Folk with Madeline MacNeil, and Barbara Hess. "Sing a Song of Sixpence" from *Girls and Boys, Come out to Play*. Music for Little People, 1991.

Dallas, Patti. "Eensy Weensy Spider" and "Sing a Song of Sixpence" from *Good Morning Sunshine*. Golden Glow Recordings, 1985.

McGrath, Bob. "Incey Wincey Spider," "Mr. Sun," "Skinnamarink" and "Skip to My Lou" from *Sing Along with Bob, Vol. 1*. Kids' Records, 1984.

McGrath, Bob. "Oh, Susanna"; "Shake My Sillies Out"; "Shortnin' Bread" and "Sing When the Spirit Says Sing" from *Sing Along with Bob, Vol. 2*. Kids' Records, 1985.

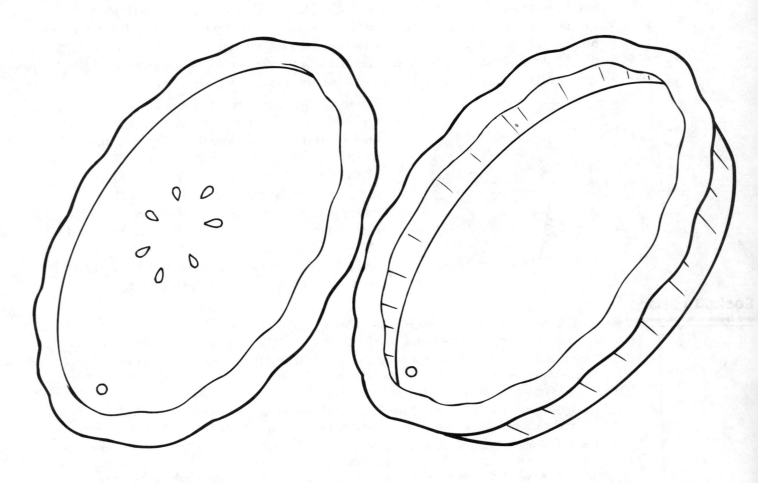

It's a SURPRISE for

_____

When: _____

Where: _____

Please come!
We'll have a SUPER time!

T

International Morse Code

Braille

I Like Toast

To the tune of "Baa, Baa, Black Sheep"
Toast with honey, toast with jam
I like toast, that's how I am.
I eat toast, every day
When I work and when I play.
Toast with honey, toast with jam
I like toast, that's how I am.

Talk About

Toast is a food that can be enjoyed anytime of the day. Some people eat toast for breakfast, some like it for sandwiches at lunch or dinner, some eat it right before bed. Ask the children when they have eaten toast. What kind of bread do they like toasted? What do they like to spread on their toast? Sing the song again using the children's suggestions for toast toppings. You might sing, "Toast with cinnamon, sugar, too. Molly likes toast and so do you."

Props/Visual Aids

Use a large sheet of chart paper to graph the children's suggestions for toast toppings. Copy, color and cut out the toast toppings on page 84, and tape them to the top of the paper. Divide the paper into columns. Cut out a piece of toast for each child using the pattern on page 84. Write the children's names on the toast and place the pieces on the chart under their choices. Which topping is the class favorite?

Tasty Toast Toppings

butter	honey	jelly	cinnamon/sugar
Erica	Ming	Jon	Steve
Rico	Juan	Min	
	Molly	Eric	
		Carlos	

Russian Tea

1 c. (240 ml) powdered instant decaffeinated tea (not lemon-flavored or sweetened)

2 c. (480 ml) orange-flavored instant breakfast powdered drink (such as Tang®)

3 c. (720 ml) sugar

1 tsp. (5 ml) cinnamon

½ tsp. (2.5 ml) cloves

Combine all the ingredients and store in an airtight container. Use two heaping tablespoons (30 ml) per cup of warm water.

To Extend This Circle Time

Bring in a toaster and have a toast party. Supply several types of bread such as whole wheat, raisin and white. Provide butter, jam, peanut butter, honey, sugar and cinnamon. Allow the children to spread their own toppings on the toast. Then sit at a table and talk as you enjoy the treat! You may wish to serve tea with the toast. Make sure the tea is cool enough to drink when served.

Songs

"I'm a Little Teapot"
"Teddy Bear, Teddy Bear"
"Tingalayo"
"Tom, Tom, the Piper's Son"
"Train Is a Comin'"
"Twinkle, Twinkle, Little Star"

Snacks

tabbouleh
tamales
tangerines
toast
tofu
tomatoes
tortellini
tortillas rolled with tuna or turkey
trail mix

Additional Activities

Set up a **terrarium** for your classroom science area. There are many good resources to help you choose plants and possibly animals to live in your terrarium. A **toad** would be a good guest.

Provide **toothpicks**, **twist ties**, colored paper **triangles** and **tissue** paper for the children to use in the art center.

Supply stamp pads with washable ink in several colors and invite the children to make **thumbprints** on paper.

Bring in several pairs of **thick** shoelaces. Show the children how to **tangle** and then **untangle** the laces. Some children may be interested in learning the steps to **tie** the laces.

Teacher for a day. Set up your dramatic play area to be a classroom. Provide a chalkboard, flannel board, table and chairs or desks. Staple several sheets of paper together to make "workbooks." Observe as the children take turns being the teacher. You may learn some surprising things!

Books to Share

Borden, Louise. *The Neighborhood Trucker.* Scholastic, Inc., 1990. Fascinated by trucks and wanting to be a trucker, Elliot watches all kinds of trucks and emulates Slim, his favorite trucker.

Crowe, Robert L. *Tyler Toad and the Thunder.* E.P. Dutton, 1980. None of the other animals' explanations for the origin of thunder seems reassuring to the frightened T. Tyler Toad as he hides in a hole waiting for the storm to pass.

Duffy, Dee Dee. *Forest Tracks.* Boyds Mills Press, 1996. Brightly colored cut-paper illustrations and simple text describe the tracks and noises of six woodland animals as well as the tire tracks of the forest ranger that lives nearby.

Fowler, Allan. *Frogs and Toads and Tadpoles, Too.* Childrens Press, 1992. Clear color photographs and simple text help explain some basic likenesses and differences between frogs and toads.

Leedy, Loreen. *Tracks in the Sand.* A Doubleday Book for Young Readers, 1993. Realistic colored pencil drawings illustrate this story of the life cycle of the loggerhead sea turtle.

Morris, Ann. *Tools.* Lothrop, Lee & Shepard Books, 1992. Colorful photographs and simple text describe tools from all over the world and the people who use them, the places they live and the cultures that surround them.

Ruis, Maria. *The Five Senses: Taste.* Barron's Educational Series, Inc., 1985. Colorful illustrations and very simple descriptions of the way some foods taste. Also includes a short scientific explanation of our sense of taste.

Tapes and CDs

McGrath, Bob. "Teddy Bear, Teddy Bear"; Tommy Thumbs Up" and "Twinkle, Twinkle" from *Songs & Games for Toddlers.* Kids' Records, 1985.

Raffi. "Thumbelina" from *Raffi in Concert with the Rise and Shine Band.* Troubadour Records, 1989.

Sharon, Lois, and Bram. "Dr. Tinker Tinker" and "Tom, Tom, the Piper's Son" from *Mainly Mother Goose: Songs and Rhymes for Merry Young Souls.* Elephant Records, 1984.

Sharon, Lois, and Bram. "Little Tommy Tucker"; "Tingalayo"; "Turkey in the Straw" and "Twinkle, Twinkle, Little Star" from *One Elephant, Deux Elephants.* Elephant Records, 1980.

Various. "I'm a Little Teapot" from *Disney's Children's Favorites, Vol. 4.* Walt Disney Records, 1990.

jam

cinnamon/sugar

butter

honey

jelly

U

International Morse Code

Braille

You and Me

To the tune of "Row, Row, Row Your Boat"
You, you, you and me
Together we make us.
Me and you and you and me,
Best friends we will be.

Talk About

Have the children join hands and sing the song together as a whole group. Use this circle time to focus on your group's identity. This may be a difficult concept for young children to understand; that the members of the group are connected and each person in the group respects and cares for the others in the group. This idea may be understood best when modeled by the adults in the environment. What other groups are the children in that can make an "us"? You might talk about family, church, neighborhoods or teams making groups of connected people. Share with the class one of Miriam Cohen's stories about school friendships such as *Best Friends*, Macmillan Publishing Company, 1971.

Props/Visual Aids

Reproduce the "Getting to Know Us" sheet on page 88 for each child in your group. Ask the children's parents to help their children complete the page and then share the responses at circle time during the week. Use an instant camera to photograph each child, and attach the picture to his or her page. Display the completed pages on an "All About Us" bulletin board or hall display. Don't forget to complete a page for yourself or other adults in the classroom!

To Extend This Circle Time

One of the things that can help create a group identity is for the class to work toward a common goal. Check with local churches or volunteer organizations to see what service projects are available in your community. Perhaps you will want to conduct a food, clothing or toy drive to help lower-income people, or you might set up regular visits to a nursing home. Be sure to supply parents with information on the project and secure permission for their child's participation.

Songs

"Ugly Duckling"
"Underwear"
"The Unicorn Song"
"Up, Up and Away"

Snacks

push-up frozen pops
ugli fruit (a type of tangelo)
Describe a snack as "ultra" or "ultimate" and eat it under the table.
upside-down cake

Additional Activities

On a rainy day, when children have brought **umbrellas**, compare the umbrellas' sizes and colors. Go for a walk in the rain! Invite the children to listen to the rain as it falls on their open umbrellas. Try to find a large umbrella for two or three people to fit under.

Check with parents and staff to see if anyone can play the **ukulele**. This small guitar-like instrument only has four strings and is quite easy to play. Ella Jenkins plays the ukulele on many of her recordings. Hawaiian music is also a good source for songs accompanied by this instrument.

Explore the spatial concept of **under** with the children. Create a special play space under a table or large box. Eat snacks or do an art project under the table. Together make a list of all the things that you do under something else.

Many professions require **uniforms**. Supply some uniform specialty catalogs for the children to look through. Bring in as many uniforms as possible for your dramatic play area. Check with parents for old uniforms they might be willing to lend. Talk about the parts of a uniform and why each might be needed. For instance: a nurse needs comfortable shoes for walking all day, a waiter needs an apron pocket for an order pad and pencil, a football player needs pads and a helmet for protection.

Children need to spend lots of time learning to tie and **untie**. Have available several shoes with laces so the children may practice. Which string do you pull to untie a bow? What if there is a double knot?

Books to Share

Cooney, Nancy Evans. *The Umbrella Day*. Philomel Books, 1989. Missy unwillingly carries her umbrella at her mother's insistence and unbelievable adventures happen making her glad she has brought it along. Soft, colorful drawings add a dream-like mood to this imaginative fantasy.

Kitamura, Satoshi. *UFO Diary*. Farrar Straus Giroux, 1989. A UFO is lost in space until it lands on a strange blue planet and makes a friend.

Monsell, Mary Elise. *Underwear!* Albert Whitman & Company, 1988. Bismark the Buffalo is grumpy until his friends teach him how to laugh and that wearing colorful underwear can be great fun.

Pinkwater, Daniel. *Roger's Umbrella*. E.P. Dutton, 1982. Roger's umbrella becomes increasingly wild and uncontrollable until he finally meets three old ladies who teach him how to talk to it.

Yashima, Taro. *Umbrella*. Viking Press, 1986. Momo cannot wait to use her birthday umbrella, but her mother insists on waiting until a rainy day. When the rain finally comes, the music it makes on the umbrella is beautiful, and Momo walks straight "like a grown-up lady!"

Tapes and CDs

Carfa, Pat. "Up, Up in the Sky" from *Songs for Sleepyheads & Out-of-Beds!* Lullaby Lady Productions, 1984.

Greg and Steve. "The Ugly Duckling" from *We All Live Together, Vol. 4*. Youngheart Records, 1980.

Penner, Fred. "Ugly Duckling" from *A House for Me*. Troubadour Records Ltd./Oak Street Music, 1985, 1991.

Roth, Kevin. "The Unicorn Song" from *The Secret Journey*. Marlboro Records, 1987.

Sharon, Lois, and Bram. "Ukulele Lady" from *Stay Tuned*. Elephant Records, 1987.

Getting to Know US

Picture goes here!

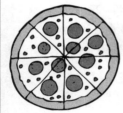

My name is _____.

I have _____ **hair**

and _____ **eyes.**

I have _____ **sister(s).**

and _____ **brother(s).**

I have a _____ **(pet).**

I like _____

_____.

I don't like _____

_____.

88

V

International Morse Code

Braille

Going on Vacation

To the tune of "The Eency Weency Spider"
I'm going on vacation, with my family.
We are going camping, there's lots to do and see.
I'll pack my toys and books, and take some extra clothes,
And we'll be gone 'til next week. I'll call you when we're home.

Talk About

Vacations are so much fun! Talk with your children about vacations they have taken. Where did they go? Whom did they see? Where did they stay? Share your own vacation stories. Are any of the children taking vacations in the near future? Take a survey of common vacation destinations. Have any of the children been to Disney World? Camping? What is the group's favorite vacation? Make a list of things you need to remember to take on vacation. What would you need for the beach? What if you went skiing?

Props/Visual Aids

Reproduce enough copies of page 92 for each child to take home. Make a display using the vacation photographs the families share. Set up a VCR in one corner of the classroom to watch segments of the vacation videos and invite the children to narrate.

To Extend This Circle Time

Plan a pretend vacation with your class. Plan your trip carefully and gather or make the props you will need. Where will you go? What will you need to take? When will you be back? A neighborhood exploration vacation is always fun. Have the children help pack knapsacks with a few books, first aid kit, tissues and, of course, a snack! You might explore a neighborhood park, read under a tree or rest in the grass. Take blank postcards for the children to draw a "having a great time, wish you were here" message.

Songs
"Fish and Chips and Vinegar"
"Red River Valley"
"Valentine's Song"
"Vegetables"

Snacks
V-8™ juice
vanilla pudding
variety of vegetables with dip
  or vinaigrette dressing

90

Additional Activities

Finger-paint with Vaseline™. This is very messy but a neat sensory experience. At first the Vaseline™ will feel cool but warm as the children play with it. Do this project with no more than four children at a time. Give each child a pair of latex gloves and place a cookie sheet in front of him or her. Put a glob of Vaseline™ on the sheet and invite the child to smear it all around. Sprinkle powdered tempera paint over the Vaseline™. When the child is done mixing the paint into the goo, place a clean sheet of paper over the cookie sheet and use a rolling pin to make a print.

Set up your dramatic play area to be a **vacation** store or travel agency. A local agency may be able to provide outdated posters of exotic destinations, as well as brochures and maps. Use the patterns on page 93 to make airplane, train or bus tickets. Your store may also sell other vacation items such as suitcases or travel clothes.

Listen to a recording that features **violin** music. Invite your high school orchestra's violin section to play for the class. Examine both a violin and a **viola**, if possible.

Set up a low net in a large space for kid **volleyball**. You may want to use a balloon or soft foam ball to play. Show the children how to serve and volley back and forth.

Vote on the children's favorite **video**. Set up a **VCR** and enjoy a video, complete with **vegetable** snacks.

Books to Share

Baker, Leslie. *Morning Beach*. Little, Brown and Company, 1990. A young girl and her mother take an early morning walk to the ocean on the first day of summer vacation, remembering the details and rituals of other years.

Brandenberg, Franz. *A Fun Weekend*. Greenwillow Books, 1991. Although their trip to the country doesn't go as planned, especially with lots of stops on the way, a family has a great deal of fun together.

Brown, Marc. *Arthur's Family Vacation*. Little, Brown and Company, 1993. Arthur is unhappy about going on vacation with his family, but he shows them how to have fun even when the rainy weather changes their plans.

Ehrlich, Fred. *A Valentine for Ms. Vanilla*. Viking, 1991. It's Valentine's Day and Ms. Vanilla's class has a great time making valentines and then reading their silly poems at the Valentine's Day party.

Florian, Douglas. *Vegetable Garden*. Harcourt Brace Jovanovich, 1991. This story tells in very simple rhyme and bright watercolor and ink pictures about a family working together in their garden, planting, weeding, watering and finally harvesting their vegetables.

French, Vivian. *Oliver's Vegetables*. Orchard Books, 1995. Brilliantly colored acrylic paintings illustrate this story of Oliver, who visits his grandfather and his wonderful garden and learns to eat lots of vegetables besides the French fried potatoes he loves.

Rockwell, Anne. *On Our Vacation*. E.P. Dutton, 1989. Throughout the Bear family's vacation, specific objects and activities relating to the settings are described in simple, clear drawings and text.

Waddell, Martin. *Sam Vole and His Brothers*. Candlewick Press, 1992. When Sam Vole goes out voling, his brothers always go too, until one day Sam finally gets to go voling all alone. Pencil and watercolor illustrations show the voles and their surroundings in humorous detail.

Tapes and CDs

Arnold, Linda. "The Vegetable Lament" from *Make Believe*. A & M Records, 1986.

Beech, Sandra. "Vegetables" from *Inch by Inch*. Attic Records Ltd., 1982.

Palmer, Hap. "Valentine's Song" from *Holiday Songs and Rhythms*. Educational Activities, Inc., 1975.

Sharon, Lois, and Bram. "Fish and Chips and Vinegar" from *Great Big Hits*. A & M Records, 1992.

Dear Parents,

We will be talking about vacations in the next few days. Can you help us by sharing photographs or videos of vacations your family has taken?

Thanks!

TICKET

_____
name

Depart from: _____
airport

Destination: _____
place

_____
date you leave home

_____
date you come home

TICKET

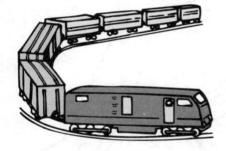

_____
name

Depart from: _____
train station

Destination: _____
place

_____
date you leave home

_____
date you come home

TICKET

_____
name

Depart from: _____

Destination: _____
place

_____
date you leave home

_____
date you come home

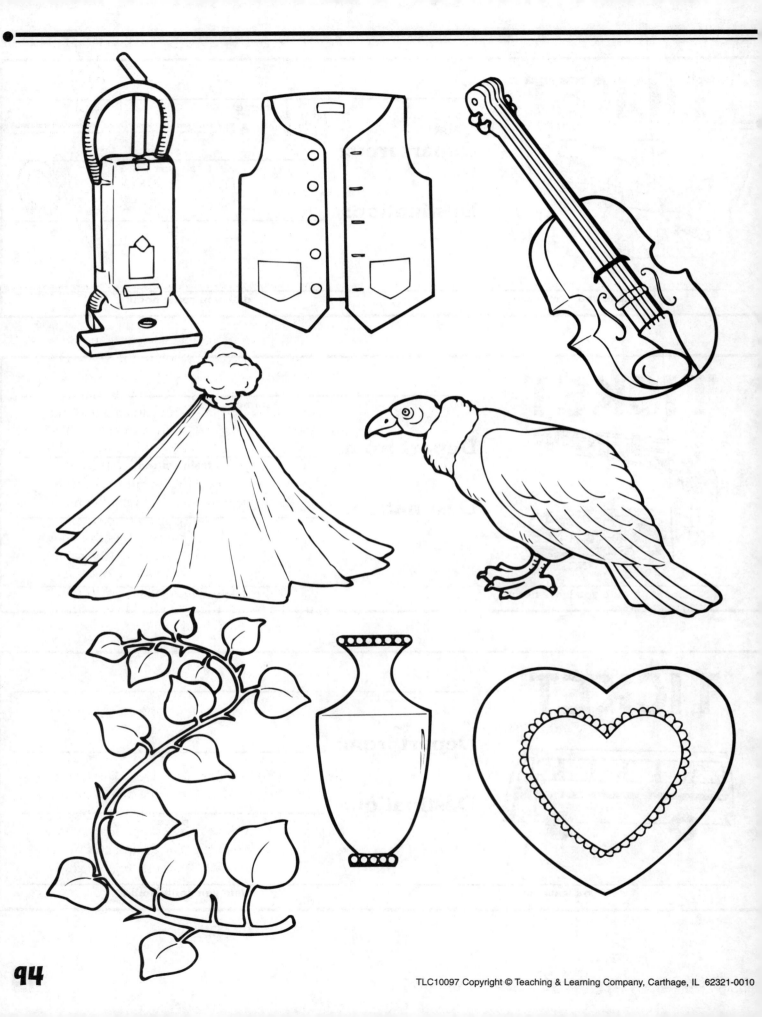

International Morse Code

Braille

Make a Wish

To the tune of "London Bridge"
Count to ten and make a wish,
Make a wish, make a wish,
Count to ten and make a wish,
Today's my wishing day.

Talk About
You can vary the words to this song by changing the action before the wish. For example, you might sing, "Turn around and make a wish" or "Clap your hands and make a wish." You can also add the names of the children in your class. "It's Hannah's wishing day." What do the children in the class wish for? List the children's responses. Talk about the differences between wishes that might come true (I want a bike for my birthday) and wishes that can't come true (I wish I were a horse). You might also discuss wishes for themselves (I wish I had 10 dollars) and wishes for other people (I wish poor people had enough food). Make a list of wishes for each kind of wish.

Props/Visual Aids
In many fairy tales, a wish is granted by the wave of a magic wand. Use the pattern on page 98 to make a magic star wand for each child. Write the children's wishes on their stars. Decorate with glue, glitter, stickers or markers and tape a pipe cleaner "handle" to each wand.

To Extend This Circle Time
Sometimes people can do things to make their wishes come true. Look carefully at the wishes on your class list. What are some actions that might make a wish happen? "We can write a note to Jimmy's mom and tell her he wants a bike for his birthday," or "I can help my mom and dad work so they will have more time to read me stories." Choose a wish for a class project. "We wish the playground had more sand." What can the class do to make this wish come true? Answers might include starting a penny collection and using the money for sand or writing a letter to the principal, the parents or custodian asking for more sand.

Songs

"I Wish I Were a Windmill"
"Pop! Goes the Weasel"
"There's a Little Wheel-a-Turning
    in My Heart"
"Walk, Walk, Walk"
"Waltzing with Bears"
"Wee Willie Winkie"
"When You Wish upon a Star"
"Willoughby, Wallaby, Woo"
"Wynken, Blynken and Nod"

Snacks

wafers
waffles
Waldorf salad
watermelon
whole wheat bread, crack-
    ers, muffins, pretzels
wontons
Gummi™ worms

Additional Activities

"Where is your **waist**?" Help every-one to find his or her waist and mea-sure it. Chart the measurements to find the most common waist size. (Be aware of any child who may be self-conscious about this measure-ment.) Do some bending and stretching exercises designed to keep waists flexible.

Learning to **walk** together in a group is an important skill for preschoolers to learn. What are the rules for your group walks? Do the children hold hands with partners? Do they have a rope with loops to grasp? Can the children walk ahead of the teachers? What about chil-dren who walk slowly or lag behind? What are the rules for corners or crossing streets? Take time to learn the rules and practice them together; then enjoy taking many walks with your group! As children become more experienced in walking as a group, you may be able to change the rules to allow more flexibility.

Weddings are a fascinating part of any culture. If a staff member, parent or family member of one of your children is planning a wedding, take the opportunity to learn more about weddings. Have any of your children been in or to a wedding? Supply some wedding clothes for your dramatic play area. Invite the children to bring in family wedding photographs or videos to share. Practice writing wedding invita-tions. It may be possible for your class to attend a wedding!

Visit a **wallpaper** store. Look at different patterns and talk with the children about in which room a certain paper might be used. The store may be able to give you discontinued sample books to use in a variety of art projects.

96

For a special treat, make a Where's the **Worm**? snack with your class. Place chocolate sandwich cookies or graham crackers in sturdy resealable bags. Crush with a rolling pin and place the crumbs in a 9" x 13" (23 x 33 cm) cake pan or on a cookie sheet. Follow the package directions to prepare a large box of chocolate instant pudding. Spread the pudding over the cookie crumbs, and then place enough Gummi™ worms (one for each child) in the pudding. Use a spoon to carefully push the worms into the pudding until they are hidden. Invite the children to dig in and find some mud, dirt and a worm for a snack!

Books to Share

Appelt, Kathi. *Watermelon Day*. Henry Holt and Company, 1996. There is a watermelon growing in the corner of the patch, and Jesse must wait patiently all summer for it to ripen and be ready for the family's annual Watermelon Day. Brilliantly colored illustrations.

Brown, Marc. *Wings on Things*. Beginner Books, 1982. Bright, simple illustrations and rhyming text show wings of many different kinds and in many different places.

Bush, John. *The Fish Who Could Wish*. Kane/Miller Book Publishers, 1991. This rhyming story tells about a fish whose wishes all come true, from a castle to fine suits and silk ties, until one day when he wishes the silliest wish he could wish.

Caines, Jeannette. *I Need a Lunch Box*. Harper & Row, 1988. A little boy wishes he could have a bright shiny lunch box like his older sister who is starting first grade.

Carlstrom, Nancy White. *Wishing at Dawn in Summer*. Little, Brown and Company, 1993. On an early morning fishing adventure, a brother and sister have different wishes. Beautiful watercolors capture a summer dawn's colors.

Field, Eugene. *Wynken, Blynken and Nod*. Scholastic, 1985. In this bedtime poem, three fishermen in a wooden shoe catch stars in their nets of silver and gold. Beautiful illustrations show a little girl and her father the real meaning of the lullaby.

Lindgren, Barbro. *A Worm's Tale*. R & S Books, 1988. Arthur is a gentleman who doesn't have any friends until he meets Charles the worm, and they become great friends, ready for fun and adventure.

Morris, Ann. *Weddings*. Lothrop, Lee & Shepard Books, 1995. Colorful and detailed photographs show weddings from around the world, and the simple text describes some of the things that often happen at weddings.

Smalls-Hector, Irene. *Jonathan and His Mommy*. Little, Brown and Company, 1992. As Jonathan and his mom explore their neighborhood, they walk in all sorts of ways–from giant steps to itsy bitsy baby steps, reggae steps to crazy crisscross steps and finally backwards steps to take them home.

Tapes and CDs

Feldman, Ellen. "Waltzing with Bears" from *Razzama Tazzama*. Ellen Feldman, 1989.

McGrath, Bob. "Wheels on the Bus"; "Willoughby, Wallaby, Woo" and "Little Wheel a Turnin'" from *Sing Along with Bob, Vol. 1*. Kids' Records, 1984.

Palmer, Hap. "Walter the Waltzing Worm" from *Walter the Waltzing Worm*. Educational Activities, Inc., 1982.

Purple Balloon Players: Sheri Huffman and John Crenshaw. "Wee Willie Winkie" from *Truckload of Fun: Sing-Alongs*. Great American Audio Corp., 1989.

Whitely, Ken, and Chris. "Walk, Walk, Walk" and "Walk Right In" from *Junior Jug Band!* Shoreline, 1981.

Various Performers. "I Wonder," "When You Wish upon a Star" and "Winnie the Pooh" from *The Disney Collection, Vol. 3*. The Walt Disney Company, 1991.

97

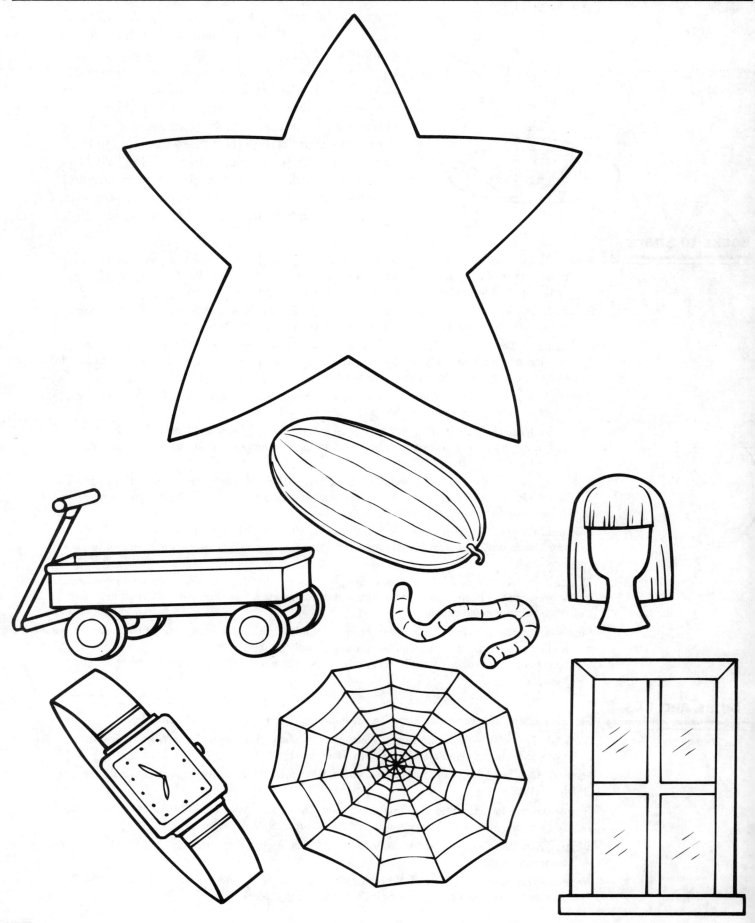

X

Going on an "X" Hunt

Have the children repeat each line in this chant.

Going on an "X" hunt
Looking for the letter "X"
Going on an "X" hunt
Where will I find it?
In my room?
Up on the ceiling?
Under the table?
In my cubbie?
Out in the hall?
Going on an "X" hunt
Looking for the letter "X"
Going on an "X" hunt
Here it is!

Talk About

"X" is a hard letter for children to learn because it has many sounds in English and is not the initial consonant in words young children frequently use. You can vary this chant in any way that works best for your children. You may wish to add clapping hands or stomping feet to the rhythm of the words or vary the clues to find the letter "X."

Props/Visual Aids

Reproduce several copies of the letter "X" on page 103. Hide an "X" in the classroom and give the children clues in the chant. Invite a child to hide an "X" and change the chant's clues to lead to the new hiding place.

To Extend This Circle Time

Make enough copies of the map and symbols on page 102 for each child. Help the children cut out the symbols and place them on their maps to create maps of the classroom. You may wish to begin this activity together by making a large group map on chart paper. After the maps are completed, give each child a paper "X" to hide somewhere in the classroom. Then each child can indicate where his or her "X" is hidden by writing an "X" on his or her map.

Songs
"The Fox Went out on a Chilly Night"
"'X' Marks the Spot"

Snacks
hot cross buns or cookies decorated with an "X"
Invite children to create "X"s with foods such as pretzel sticks, carrot sticks, etc.
Trix™ cereal
Twix™ candy bar

Additional Activities

Take a walk around your building and find all the **exit** signs. How many are there? Where are they placed? Why? Provide the children with construction paper and markers and an exit sign to use as a model. Invite the children to make their own exit signs to use at home.

An **X ray** can take a picture of what is inside our bodies. If you have any parents who work in the health care field, ask if they might obtain some X-ray photographs for your class to view. Can the children identify which part of the body is in the X-ray picture? Invite the children to feel the bones in their bodies that are pictured in the X ray. Make an "X-ray picture" of each child's hand. First, trace around his or her hand on a piece of paper. Then with finger paint, carefully paint the inside of his or her hand. Ask the child if he or she can feel the bones in his or her fingers as you smooth the paint over them. Carefully place the painted hand over the traced drawing to make a print.

Plan an **exciting** event for your children. It may be a field trip, a party or a special visitor. Talk about other times that they have been excited. How did they show their excitement? Take turns acting excited. Be prepared for a silly and noisy time!

Large **excavating** equipment is fascinating to some children. Bring out any toy diggers, scoops and shovels that you may have for your sandbox or sensory table. Bury some "treasures" in the sand for the children to discover as they are excavating. Plan a field trip to a nearby gravel pit, quarry or construction site to see excavation equipment in action.

Exercise! In an open, carpeted area invite the children to join you in some warm-up stretches. How high can you reach? Extend arms and turn from side to side. March in place and then try some jumping jacks. Can the children feel their hearts beating faster? Have the children touch the floor, walk out with their hands (feet are stationary) and do some push-ups for strength. Check with your library or video store for exercise tapes for children.

Books to Share

Brown, Margaret Wise. *The Diggers*. Hyperion Books for Children, text © 1958, illustrations © 1995. Verses describe the holes that a mole, dog, worm and rabbit dig, but none can compare with the excavating work of a man and his steam shovel. Brilliantly colored oil paintings.

Bunting, Eve. *Red Fox Running*. Clarion Books, 1993. Rhyming text and beautiful paintings follow the experiences of red fox as it searches across a wintry landscape for food for its family.

Lillegard, Dee. *Sitting in My Box*. E.P. Dutton, 1989. A rhythmically told story of a boy whose box gets more and more crowded with all the animals who invite themselves in, until a hungry flea comes along.

Spier, Peter. *The Fox Went out on a Chilly Night*. Dell Publishing, 1961. This folk song about a fox looking for food for his family is illustrated with watercolor and ink and includes music for voice, piano and guitar.

Wallace, Karen. *Red Fox*. Candlewick Press, 1994. Accurately and beautifully illustrated with vivid colored pencils, this book has simple text and added notes about the behavior and biology of foxes.

Watson, Wendy. *Fox Went out on a Chilly Night*. Lothrop, Lee & Shepard, 1994. Bright illustrations help retell this familiar folk song of the fox finding dinner for his wife and 10 kits. Also includes notes for the traditional tune.

Tapes and CDs

Peter, Paul, and Mary. "The Fox" from *Peter, Paul and Mommy, Too*. Warner Brothers, 1993.

Sesame Street Muppets. "'X' Marks the Spot" from *Letters and Numbers*. Sesame Street Records, 1981.

Sesame Street Muppets. "'X' Marks the Spot" from *The Muppet Alphabet Album*. Sesame Street Records/Golden, 1971.

Sharon, Lois, and Bram. "XYZinnamrink" from *Sing A to Z*. Elephant Records/A & M Records, 1990.

Sterben, Willie. "The Fox in a Box" from *Chickens in My Hair*. Singing Toad Productions, 1986.

Map of My Room

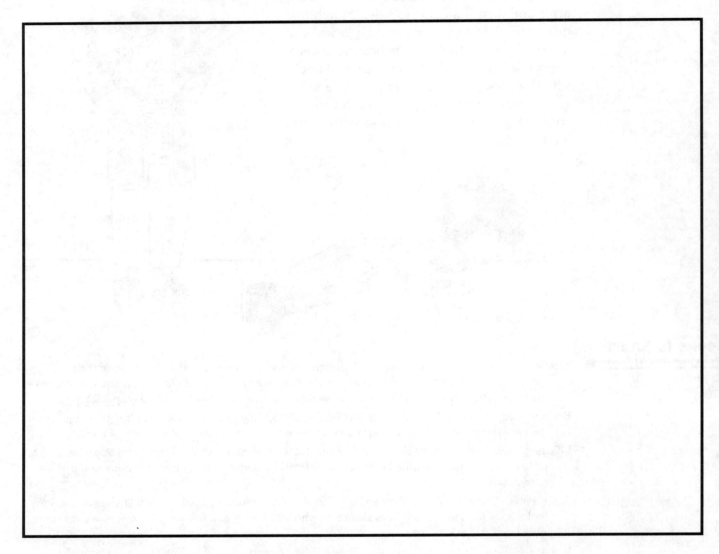

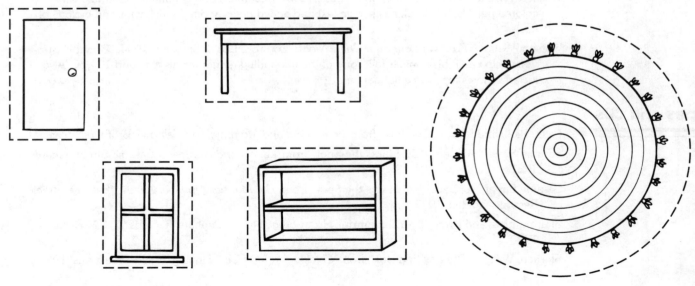

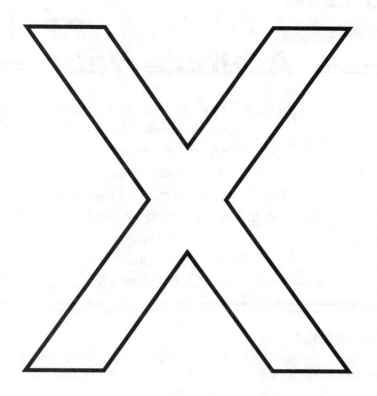

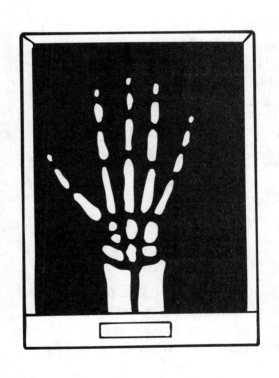

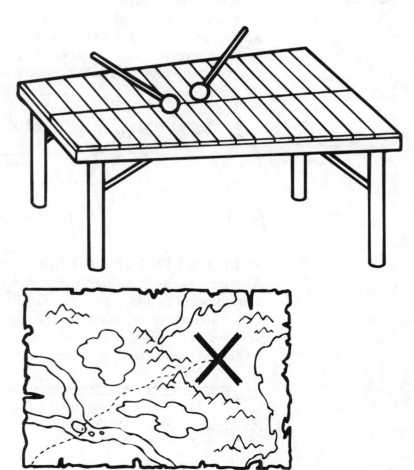

Y

International Morse Code

Braille

A Whole Year

January

December

To the tune of "Good Night, Ladies"
January, February,
March and April,
May and June,
The first six months of the year.
Repeat melody starting at the beginning
July, August,
September, October.
Finally remember November and December!

Talk About

A year is a very long time for a young child! Help the children in your class remember the order of the months of the year with this simple song. Talk about what special events or holidays might fall during certain months of the year. Which months are cold or warm?

Props/Visual Aids

Reproduce and cut out the months on pages 106 and 107, and have the children work in groups to color them. Invite 12 children to stand in a row holding the month names in order. Have each child hold up his or her month as the class says the chant together. Repeat until every child has had a chance to participate.

To Extend This Circle Time

A common activity during circle time is to "do the calendar." It is important for children to begin to understand the passing of time from day to day and season to season. Often however, calendar time becomes simple memorization and rote learning. Try using a simple time line for a calendar so the children can easily see yesterday, today and tomorrow as a continuum.

Songs

"Yankee Doodle Dandy"
"Yankee Doodle"
"Yellow Submarine"

Snacks

yam (Raw yams can be peeled and
    cut like carrot sticks.)
yeast bread
yogurt
egg yolk

Additional Activities

Yo-yos are fun to watch but require more coordination than most preschoolers possess. Do any of your parents have a hidden talent for yo-yos? Check with staff and older siblings, too, for a possible yo-yo demonstration.

Introduce your class to some simple **yoga** exercises. Check with a local fitness center or borrow a yoga videotape to find appropriate exercises and stretches for children. Wear comfortable clothing and place mats on the floor. Be sure to stretch out and warm up your muscles before attempting to demonstrate the lotus position!

Add scraps of **yarn** to your art center. Cut the yarn in 1" to 2" (2.5 to 5 cm) pieces. Place glue diluted with water in a shallow bowl and provide paintbrushes for spreading the glue. Children can use the yarn to add texture and color to their art creations.

Use a **yardstick** to measure large items in your classroom. Measure the children, too! How many of them are taller than the yardstick?

Make a list of questions that the children would answer with a "**Yes**!" Read the list back to the group and invite them to answer with a chorus of "yesses." "Would you like pizza and ice cream for dinner?" Then think of some questions they would like to have their parents answer with a "yes." "Would you read me a story? Can we buy a puppy?" During the day's activities, have everyone say "yes" as often as possible and count the number of "yesses" you hear.

Books to Share

Anholt, Catherine. *Tom's Rainbow Walk.* Little, Brown and Company, 1989. Tom had a hard time choosing a color for the sweater Grandma wants to knit, until in a dream he follows a big ball of yarn all around the garden meeting different animals who help him solve his dilemma.

Carlstrom, Nancy White. *How Do You Say It Today, Jesse Bear?* Macmillan Publishing Company, 1992. Rhyming text and detailed illustrations describe Jesse Bear's activities month by month from January to December.

Halsey, Megan. *Jump for Joy: A Book of Months.* Bradbury Press, 1994. Bouncy, alliterative text and bright, paper sculpture illustrations show a playful activity for each month of the year, from jumping for joy in January to doing a dance in December.

Hariton, Anca. *Egg Story.* Dutton's Children's Books, 1992. From a white spot on a golden yolk to a wet and weary chick that has broken out of its shell, each stage of growth inside an egg is simply and accurately portrayed in simple text and clear drawings.

Lillegard, Dee. *My Yellow Ball.* Dutton's Children's Books, 1993. Five times, when a girl throws her yellow ball, her imagination takes it faraway to jungles, deserts and finally, outer space, but it always returns.

Lillie, Patricia. *When This Box Is Full.* Greenwillow Books, 1993. Each month of the year, a child adds something to fill a box, including a red foil heart in February and toasted pumpkin seeds in October. Hand-colored black and white photographs.

Maestro, Betsy, and Giulio. *Through the Year with Harriet.* Crown Publishers, Inc., 1985. This book follows Harriet the elephant through the 12 months of the year as she engages in many activities in all kinds of weather.

Raschka, Chris. *Yo! Yes?* Orchard Books, 1993. Simple, one- or two-word sentences show two boys meeting on a street and becoming tentative and then emphatic friends.

Tapes and CDs

Bishop, Heather. "Yakety Yak" from *A Duck in New York City.* Oak Street Music, 1990.

King's Singers, The. "Yellow Submarine" from *Kids' Stuff.* EMI Records Ltd., 1986.

Various. "Yankee Doodle" from *Disney's Children's Favorites, Vol. 2.* Walt Disney Productions, 1979.

Various. "Yankee Doodle" and "Yankee Doodle Dandy" from *Patriotic Songs & Marches.* Kimbo, 1991.

January

February

March

April

May

June

July

August

September

October

November

December

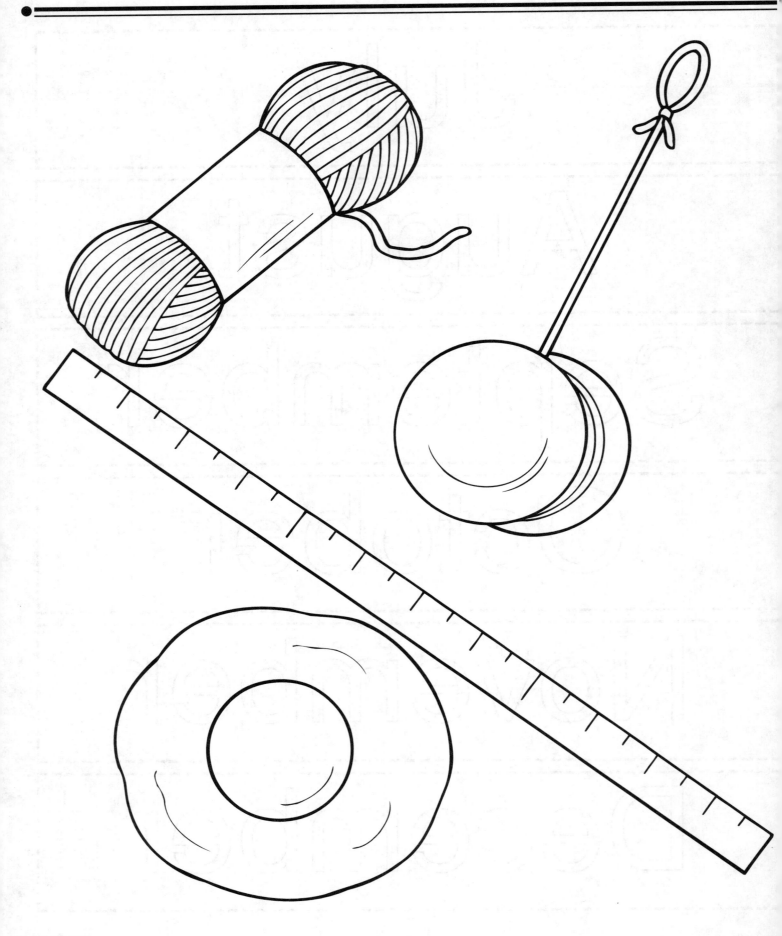

108

Z

International Morse Code

Braille

Z Song

To the tune of "I've Been Working on the Railroad"
"Z" likes to be the end, the last letter in line
"Z" follows all the rest, and likes it there just fine
"Z" is busy buzzing by
Going on its way
Following the other letters
The alphabet's done, hooray!

Talk About

"Z" is the last letter of the alphabet. The song says "Z" likes being last. There is always emphasis on being "first"; talk about some reasons or times the children may want to be last. When is it good to be last? If you are having a good time playing, would you want to be the last to leave the playground? Would you like to be the last person in your house to go to bed? What does *saving the best for last* mean?

Props/Visual Aids

The caboose is the last car on a train. Reproduce, color and cut out the caboose pattern on page 111. Write on the caboose the important jobs the last person in line must be sure to do. These might include closing the classroom door, making sure everyone is in line and turning out the lights. Have the children take turns being the last in line, carrying the caboose card and performing the important "last person" jobs.

To Extend This Circle Time

Play a game where it is good to be last such as Musical Chairs. You may wish to substitute hand or paper towels on the floor for chairs. The children may stand on the towels when the music stops, and after each pause, remove one towel. The last child remaining wins!

Give the children a snack consisting of a mixture of things, such as different types of dry cereal or cups of mixed fruit. Invite the children to eat their snacks, saving whatever part they like the best for last.

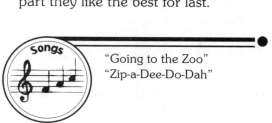

Songs
"Going to the Zoo"
"Zip-a-Dee-Do-Dah"

Snacks
pizza
ziti
zucchini bread or muffins
zwieback toast

Additional Activities

Help the children learn how to **zip** and unzip. Place clothing with zippers in your dramatic play area. When dressing for outside play, assign the children partners to help with zipping up their friends' sweaters and coats.

Take a field trip to the **zoo**. Before you go, talk about the animals you might see. Place plastic zoo animal models in your block area or sand table.

With special scissors that create a **zigzag,** cut shapes from scraps of colorful construction paper. Invite the children to create zigzag collages by gluing the shapes on another piece of paper.

Zany is another word to describe something that is silly or comical. Many of the "Z" songs are zany. Plan a Zany Day activity with your class. You might have a beach party in the middle of winter or a daytime slumber party. Invite your children to come up with more zany ideas.

Do the children know their **zip** codes? How many different zip codes are represented by the children in your class? If you have several zip codes, write them on large cards and show them to group the children when lining up or moving to a new activity. Post a community map with the school and children's homes labeled, and the borders for the different zip code areas.

Books to Share

Barbour, Karen. *Little Nino's Pizzeria*. Harcourt Brace Jovanovich, 1987. Tony loves to help his father do everything from kneading pizza dough to carrying out dirty dishes at their small family restaurant, but everything changes when Little Nino's Pizzeria becomes a much fancier place.

Dowell, Philip. *Zoo Animals*. Aladdin Books, 1991. Clear photographs, detailed drawings and simple text introduce the elephant, camel, monkey, zebra, parrot, tiger, snake and penguin.

Hendrick, Mary Jean. *If Anything Ever Goes Wrong at the Zoo*. Harcourt Brace Jovanovich, 1993. After Leslie tells the zookeepers to send the animals to her house should anything go wrong at the zoo, a series of zoo emergencies results in some unusual houseguests for Leslie and her mom.

Omerod, Jan. *When We Went to the Zoo*. Lothrop, Lee & Shepard, 1990. On a trip to the zoo, two children pet, ride and look at many exotic animals and then find something wonderful in the ordinary. Detailed drawings with insets show the animals in varied environments and actions.

Pulver, Robin. *Mrs. Toggle's Zipper*. Four Winds Press, 1990. When Mrs. Toggle's zipper sticks and traps her inside her coat, everyone in the school tries to free her but with little success. Humorous watercolors illustrate her predicament.

Tapes and CDs

Diamond, Charlotte. "Zing, Zing, Zing" from *Ten Carrot Diamond*. Hug Bug Records, 1985.

Greg and Steve. "Zip-a-Dee-Do-Dah" from *Playing Favorites*. Youngheart Records, 1991.

McGrath, Bob, and Katharine Smithrim. "Zoom Zoom Zoom" from *Songs and Games for Toddlers*. Kids' Records, 1985.

Raffi. "Going to the Zoo" from *The Singable Songs Collection*. Shoreline/A & M Records, 1988.

Sesame Street Muppets. "Zippy Zoomers" from *Letters and Numbers*. Sesame Street Records, 1981.

Sharon, Lois, and Bram. "Going to the Zoo" from *Sharon, Lois, and Bram's Elephant Show Record*. Elephant Records/A & M Records, 1986.

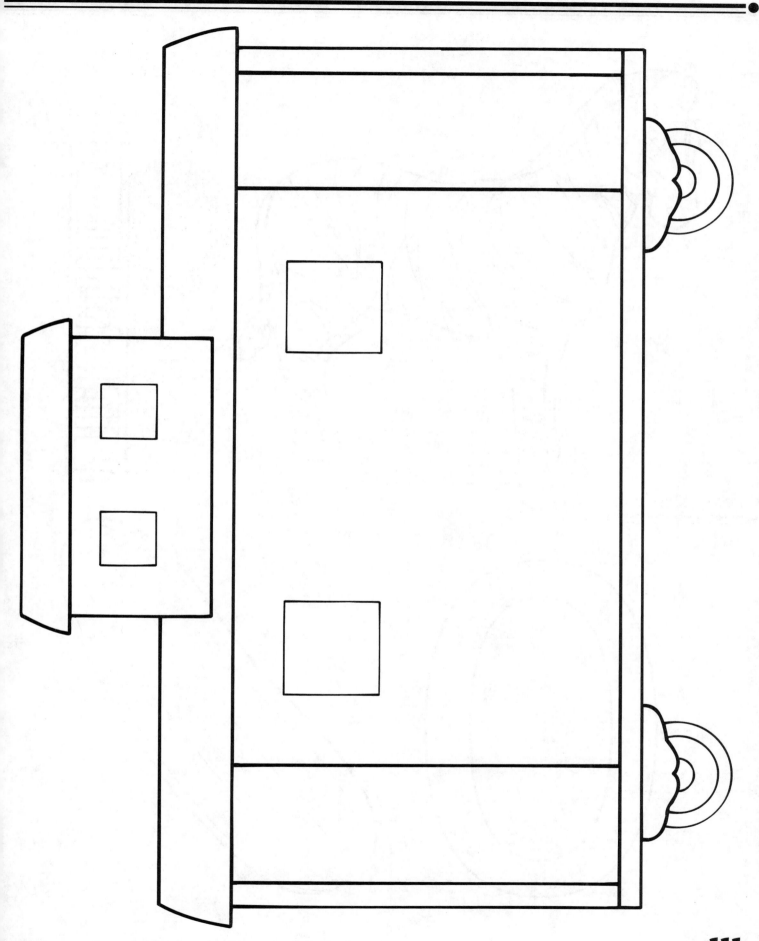

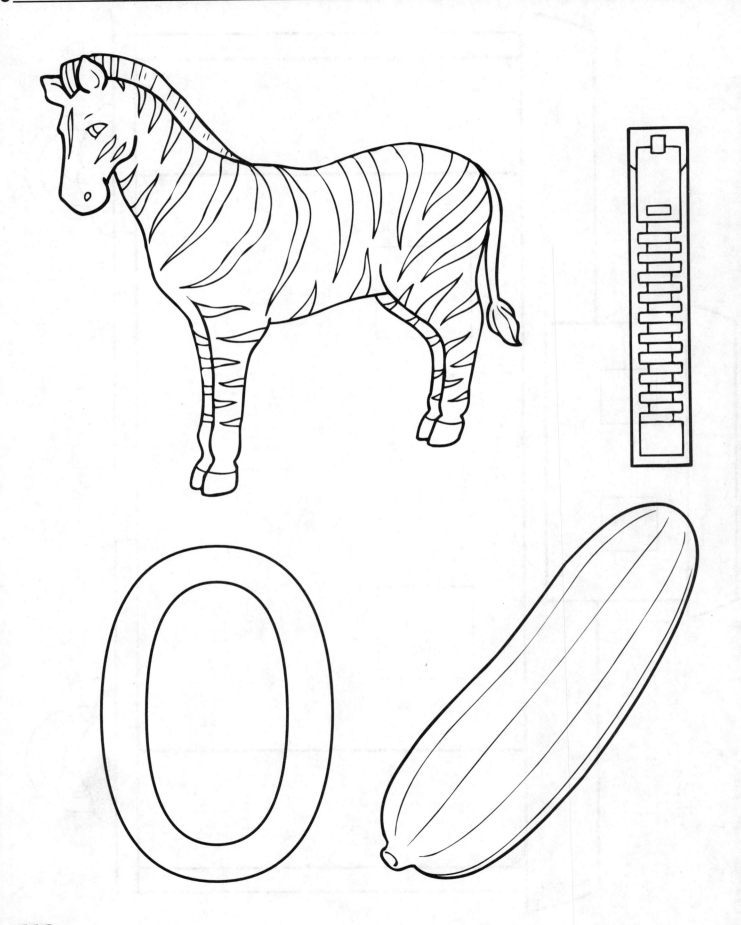